Grandma's *Rāmāyaṇa*

By Chandrakala S. Kammath

Mata Amritanandamayi Center
San Ramon, California, USA

Grandma's *Rāmāyaṇa*
By Chandrakala S. Kammath
Translated from Malayalam into English by Rajani Menon
Illustrations by Dinesh

Published By:
Mata Amritanandamayi Center
P.O. Box 613
San Ramon, CA 94583-0613, USA

In India:
www.amritapuri.org
inform@amritapuri.org

In Europe:
www.amma-europe.org

In US:
www.amma.org

Preface

"If we assimilate the message of the *Rāmāyaṇa*,
we can be liberated from all sorrows of life."

—Amma

If people are to be righteous and cultured, noble values must be instilled in them from a young age. The easiest way to do this is by familiarizing children with stories of God. Tales of the divine play of Śrī Rāma, Śrī Kṛṣṇa and other divine incarnations help us understand *dharma* (code of righteous conduct). Their lives convey how one may conduct oneself righteously.

Children today are becoming increasingly less conversant with the values that *Sanātana Dharma* (Hinduism) espouses, principles of spirituality, and the biographies of divine incarnations. This is why we have translated and published *Grandma's Rāmāyaṇa*, which was serialised every month in the Malayāḷam edition of *Matruvani. Grandma's Rāmāyaṇa* — based on *Ādhyātma Rāmāyaṇa* by Ezhuttacchan, the father of Malayāḷam — was written by Chandrakala S. Kammath and translated into English by Rajani Menon. The style is engaging and easily understandable.

In the past, it was grandmothers who narrated stories of God to young children. This is the inspiration behind this book, in which a grandmother narrates the *Rāmāyaṇa* to her young grandson, Uṇṇi; hence the title of this book. Here's a suggestion: gather all the children in the house together at least once a week, and read to them a chapter of *Grandma's Rāmāyaṇa*. Doing this regularly would be the best service you can render future generations.

Listen to (or read) the stories of Śrī Rāmacandra and reflect upon them. Doing so promotes spiritual growth. The *Rāmāyaṇa* contains hymns in praise of God, stories of devotees, and pointers on righteous conduct. By reading these stories, our children will grow up to be ideal citizens and ethical human beings. We hope that *Grandma's Rāmāyaṇa* fulfils these aspirations. We offer this book to Amma with the humble prayer that She showers Her blessings on it and on its readers.

Publisher

Contents

1. What Grandma Said

Uṇṇi and his friends opened the gate and trooped into the courtyard. They had just returned from school. Grandma, sitting in the open veranda of the house, asked, "My dear children, you're back so soon?"

"We have come to pluck flowers for the *Ōṇam pūkkaḷam.*[1] We don't have any classes tomorrow."

"You're all perspiring and panting," said Grandma.

"Yes! We raced each other from school and stopped only when we got here," Uṇṇi said.

1 Ōṇam is Kerala's harvest festival. A pūkkaḷam is a flower mandala (circular floral arrangement).

Grandma laughed and said, "I shall make sweet lemonade for all of you. Rest here in the veranda."

"Why don't we pluck flowers until then?" asked Uṇṇi. "We can collect enough flowers before you return."

Grandmother went inside. There were many varieties of flowers in the garden, though not as many as there used to be in her childhood. Still, there was enough for the children to make a small and intricate pūkkaḷam.

When she returned with the lemonade, she saw that the children had collected two basketfuls of flowers. She served them lemonade, which they happily sipped. Grandmother sat down and took up the *Rāmāyaṇa*, which she had been reading.

One of Uṇṇi's friends asked, "Grandma, why do you read this old tale every day? Everyone knows the story. Don't you get bored?"

Grandma smiled at the child and gently chucked his chin. "Would you say no if I offered you sweet lemonade tomorrow?"

"No," the children shouted. "We want to drink it every day!"

"But you have already tasted it. Would you still want it tomorrow?" Grandma asked.

"Grandma, we will never say no to your lemonade!"

Grandma said, "The books containing stories of God and the principles underlying them might seem boring and old fashioned until you get to know them. Then they begin to taste like nectar. You will never get enough of it."

The children looked at each other. "We don't understand, Grandma," said one.

Grandma stretched her legs and said, "Children, what you learn in school are scientific facts that can be proved by your brain and experienced by your sense organs. God is beyond man's intelligence. No experiment can prove the existence of God, the divine consciousness that pervades this universe."

The children remained silent for a while. One of them asked, "How then can we learn about God?"

Grandma smiled fondly at him. "There are many ways to experience the divine energy, which God is. Let me give you a few examples. Look at the flowers you have collected. How beautiful and colourful they are! They are in different shapes and sizes and have unique fragrances, too. One species of flower will never bloom on another plant.

"In school, you might dissect a flower, find out what gives it colour, and what it is made of. But how did it come into being? What power breathed life into it?

"Who created the seasons? There is an unseen power behind the natural rhythm of this universe. We are all living in this world according to the will of that great power."

The children listened, wide-eyed with wonder.

Pointing some distance away, Grandma continued, "My dear children, do you see that huge banyan tree over there?"

The kids nodded their heads.

"Have you seen its tiny seed? How did such a huge tree emerge from such a tiny seed? Who created the seed?

"There are so many other miracles in the world: the sun, moon, stars, great mountains, vast oceans, and all the creatures in the world. All of them live as if programmed to follow certain behavioural patterns. Who bestowed on them their tendencies?

"There is an infinite and eternal power governing the universe. We call that great power God. We are unable to see God with our human eyes, but God, or that primal energy, is within each one of us. He is present in each atom.

"Isn't water the same, whether it's a bubble on the ocean's surface or a huge wave? In the same manner, divine consciousness is present in the biggest and the smallest object in the world."

The children were listening attentively.

Grandma paused for a moment, and looked fondly at the children. She then said, "We call this divine consciousness our Self or *Ātmā*. We call it goodness. God is truth, love and compassion. One whose life is filled with truth, love and compassion has divine qualities in him.

"When elders tell you not to lie, not to hurt others, and to be kind and sympathetic to others, they are trying to mould you into noble people, into becoming the children of God.

"So, apart from your school studies, you must also read the *Purāṇas,* the tales of gods and goddesses. We must read the stories of *mahātmās* (spiritually illumined souls) like Śrī Rāmakṛṣṇa Paramahamsa, Śrī Nārāyaṇa Guru, Swāmi Vivēkānanda, Rāmaṇa Maharṣi and Amma, the hugging saint from India. Reading about them can help us understand God more easily. Read these books during your vacations."

"We will, Grandma," the children said enthusiastically.

Grandmother hugged and kissed each one of them.

Uṇṇi asked, "Grandma, if I bring my friends over during the holidays, will you tell us stories from the *Rāmāyaṇa* and *Mahābhārata*?

"Of course," Grandma beamed. "That's what I'm here for!"

2. Story of Vālmīki

Grandma leaned against the half wall of the veranda. Lunch was over. She picked up the newspaper. All the others at home were resting after a heavy lunch. Uṇṇi had never seen Grandma sleep during the day. She would either be cooking in the kitchen or reading. She would also tell Uṇṇi many stories. Or she would sit somewhere quietly, with eyes closed. Her lips would be moving silently. Uṇṇi knew that Grandma was praying then.

Uṇṇi ran up to her and nestled in her lap. Grandma put the paper down and hugged him. "What is it, Uṇṇi? What does my sweet child want?"

"Grandma, you must tell me something."

"What about, son?"

"Today, our Malayāḷam teacher told us to write about Sage Vālmīki. She said that it was Vālmīki who wrote the *Rāmāyaṇa*. I don't know anything about him, and I don't really know the *Rāmāyaṇa* either."

"Is that all?" Grandma smiled happily. "I will tell you about Vālmīki and about the *Rāmāyaṇa* he wrote. I will tell you all the stories in the *Rāmāyaṇa*. It is too big to absorb in one day."

"All right." Uṇṇi was relieved. He knew his grandmother would save the day. "Tell me about Vālmīki first,

DINESH

because I have to write about him in my own words and show the teacher my writing tomorrow."

Grandma started speaking slowly and softly. "When we hear the tale of Sage Vālmīki, we will understand how a bad man can turn into a wise and compassionate human being. Listen well, Uṇṇi. His name was Ratnākaran. As a child, he got into the company of bad people. He started waylaying people and stealing their belongings. He became a fierce robber. He grew up, got married and had many children. He continued robbing people to take care of his family. He did not feel bad at all about stealing money and other possessions from others. He was indeed a terrible man.

"One day, Sage Nārada was walking through the forest with other hermits. Ratnākaran ambushed them and said, 'O sages! Give me all that you have. I shall not release you until I have everything you own. If you value your lives, give me everything.'

"The sages were not perturbed. They asked him, 'What is your name?'

"'Ratnākaran.'

"'You are committing a great sin,' said one of the sages.

"'What sin?' Ratnākaran asked. 'I steal for the sake of my family. How can that be a sin? What other means do I have to take care of my family?'

"Sage Nārada asked him, 'Are your wife and children prepared to share the burden of sin you're incurring?'

"Ratnākaran did not say anything.

"Nārada said, 'Go home and ask your wife and children, and return with the answer. We shall wait here for you. Sages keep their word.'

"The robber ran home. When he saw his wife, he asked her, 'You will share the burden of my sins, won't you?'

"His wife immediately said, 'No! Why should I share your sins and suffer in hell? You can be sure that I will never share your sins!'

"His children also refused to share his sins.

"Ratnākaran returned to where the sages were waiting for him and begged forgiveness of them. The sages advised him to chant 'Marā... marā...' continuously and to meditate upon the word."

Uṇṇi was listening intently. Grandma asked him, "When you chant 'Marā... marā...' continuously, what does it become?"

Uṇṇi closed his eyes and repeated, "Marā... marām... marāma... rāma... rāma... rāma..." He soon became breathless. "Grandma, it becomes Rāma!" he said, smiling in delight. "Wow, what an idea!"

"Ratnākaran sat underneath a tree, closed his eyes, started chanting the mantra, and soon became absorbed in deep meditation. He was not aware of the passing of days, months and years. His mind was steeped in Lord Rāma. Termites began to build their mound around him. In Sānskṛt, termites are called 'Vālmīkam.' After many years, Sage Nārada and the other hermits passed that way again. They heard the constant chant of 'Rāma... Rāma... Rāma... Rāma... Rāma... Rāma...' emanating from the huge termite mound. They broke open the mound and pulled out Ratnākaran. As he had emerged from the vālmīkam, he was named 'Vālmīki.'"

Uṇṇi looked at Grandma with eyes wide in wonder. "Grandma, Vālmīki must have been a great sage!" he exclaimed.

"Yes, Uṇṇi." Grandma said, enjoying the excitement of her young listener.

"Lord Rāma and Vālmīki were contemporaries. The *Rāmāyaṇa* comprises 24,000 verses. It is said to be the first epic poem, and Vālmīki is regarded as the first epic poet."

Uṇṇi's eyes were shining with joy. Grandma said, "Enough for the day, Uṇṇi. Go and write about Vālmīki and bring the story back to me. Grandma shall correct the grammar, if there are mistakes."

Uṇṇi got up. "Alright, Grandma, but promise to tell me the story of *Rāmāyaṇa* from tomorrow onwards."

Grandma nodded her head. Uṇṇi kissed both of Grandma's cheeks and ran inside.

*"**Even a very bad person can become wise and kind through satsang.[2] Seek the company of good people. Their conversation will quiet your mind and open your heart. Hearken to their words of wisdom. Adhere to their words. Your life will become filled with goodness. Through satsang and the practice of noble teachings, anyone can become an ideal human being.***

2 'Communion with Truth.' Satsang includes discourses on spiritual topics or keeping the company of the holy.

3. Birth of Śrī Rāma

Uṇṇi hurriedly closed his textbook and ran up to Grandma. From the eager look on his face, she knew that Uṇṇi was impatient to listen to the *Rāmāyaṇa*. He said, "Grandma, I've finished my homework. I've also prepared for tomorrow's examination."

"Good boy! Now, listen well. Daśaratha was a great and powerful king in the *Sūryavamśa* (solar dynasty). He ruled Ayōdhyā ably, and during his peaceful reign, the land prospered. His subjects revered him. But the king was sad. Do you know why, Uṇṇi? There wasn't an heir to the throne. Though he had three wives — Kausalyā, Kaikēyī and Sumitrā — none of them had borne him a son."

"Oh, that's sad!" said Uṇṇi. "How much the poor king would have loved a baby to play with."

Grandma continued, "Daśaratha prostrated at the feet of his Guru Vasiṣṭha and said, 'I'm very sad that I cannot have a son. Please advise me on how I can beget an heir to the throne.'

"'Invite Sage Ṛṣyaśṛnga to perform the *Putrakāmēṣṭi Yāgā*,'[3] replied Guru Vasiṣṭha."

---

3 A sacred rite performed to beget children.

"Who's Ṛṣyaśṛnga?" asked Uṇṇi.

"He was a great sage who brought rain to the drought-ridden land of Anga. I shall tell you his story some other time."

Uṇṇi nodded his head.

"Ṛṣyaśṛnga was invited to Ayōdhyā, where he conducted a grand *yajña* (ritual fire sacrifice) by the banks of River Sarayū. As he was pouring oblations into the fire pit, the God of Fire arose from the pit. He was holding a pot of *pāyasam* (sweet pudding) in his hands. He said, 'O great king, this pāyasam is divine. Give a portion each to your wives and they shall bear you sons.'

"With great reverence, Daśaratha accepted the pot from the hands of the fire god. He divided the pāyasam into two and gave one share each to Kausalyā and Kaikēyī. They, in turn, divided what they received, and each gave half her share to Sumitrā. All three queens conceived. The first to be born was the son of Kausalyā. Born under the *Puṇartam* star, He was Lord Rāmacandra. Kaikēyī's son, Bharata, was born the day after under the *Pūyam* star. On the third day, Sumitrā gave birth to twins, under the *Āyilyam* star. They were named Lakṣmaṇa and Śatrughna. The king, his queens and the whole kingdom rejoiced at the birth of the four baby boys."

Uṇṇi clutched his Grandma's hand and whispered, "I know why the twins were born."

"Why?"

"Because Kausalyā and Kaikēyī had each given half their share to Sumitrā."

Grandma laughed, pleased with her grandson's attentiveness. "Yes, Uṇṇi. There is one very important thing we must understand from this episode: we must always share what we have with others, even special gifts and ice creams. Sharing makes us more caring and considerate. Now, let me tell you the secret behind the birth of the four boys."

"Is there a secret?" Uṇṇi inched closer to his grandmother. His head rested gently on her chest. Grandma stroked her grandson's soft hair as she continued.

"Yes, there is. There was a cruel *asura* (demon) king named Rāvaṇa who ruled Lanka. Once, he observed a great penance for many years to propitiate Lord Brahmā. Pleased with him, the Lord appeared before him and encouraged Rāvaṇa to ask for any boon.

"Rāvaṇa said, 'Make me Lord of the whole world. Only a human being should be able to kill me.'

"Rāvaṇa knew that no puny human could match his immense strength and skill. Brahmā granted him the boon. Rāvaṇa conquered the three worlds and started ruling over them as he fancied. Many of his actions were unjust. Even the celestial beings became afraid of him. The sages were no longer able to perform *tapas* (austerities) or fire rituals. Rāvaṇa had become invincible. He became arrogant.

"Unable to bear the burden of his wickedness, Bhūmidēvi (Goddess of the Earth) and other celestial beings sought the protection of Lord Viṣṇu, Sustainer of the Universe. He listened to their tale of sorrow and comforted them: 'Do not worry. Go back in peace. I shall incarnate on earth to destroy the evil Rāvaṇa and his race of asuras. I shall be born as the son of King Daśaratha of Ayōdhyā.'"

Uṇṇi was listening intently to his grandmother's words.

She continued, "Śrī Rāmacandra was the incarnation of Lord Viṣṇu. Lakṣmaṇa, Bharata and Śatrughna were partial incarnations of the Lord, too. The celestial beings were born as monkeys. Lord Rāmacandra was born in this world to kill the asuras and to cleanse the world of evil, to bring humanity back to the path of righteousness."

Uṇṇi's face was shining, and his eyes reflected awe and wonder.

Grandma hugged Uṇṇi tightly and said, "God is always compassionate, Uṇṇi. When wickedness flourishes, the Lord incarnates to destroy evil and to restore righteousness. The Lord had incarnated before as Matsya (the divine fish), Kūrma (the divine tortoise) and Varāha (the divine boar) when evil swept over the world. Here, He incarnated as Śrī Rāmacandra, the personification of righteousness."

“ ***If an evil person acquires strength, he will wreak disaster on the world. The only way to resist such evil is to take refuge in the Lord. Even if the wicked are very strong, God will incarnate to destroy them on hearing the prayers of the noble.***

4. Arrival of Viśvāmitra

Śrīkuṭṭi, Uṇṇi's younger sister, was lying in Grandma's lap. Uṇṇi ran up to them and asked, "What happened to Śrīkuṭṭi, Grandma?"

Grandma replied, "She has a slight fever. Let her sleep in my lap. Poor child! She might cry if we lay her down on the bed."

"I want to hear more stories from the *Rāmāyaṇa*." Uṇṇi cuddled close to his grandmother. "Śrīkuṭṭi is asleep. Can you tell me more stories of Rāma?

"Where did I stop, Uṇṇi?" Grandma asked. "Oh yes, Rāma, Lakṣmaṇa, Bharata and Śatrughna were born. I also told you the secret of their birth. All right, let's continue.

"The four princes, the sons of King Daśaratha, became dear not just to their parents, but also to the subjects of Ayōdhyā. As they grew up, they never fought or argued with each other. They remained united in thought and deed. And yet, there was something special about their relationship. Rāma and Lakṣmaṇa were inseparable as were Bharata and Śatrughna. Perhaps it was because Sumitrā had eaten half of both Kausalyā's and Kaikēyī's share of the pāyasam. From Kausalyā's share of the pāyasam came Lakṣmaṇa, and from Kaikēyī's,

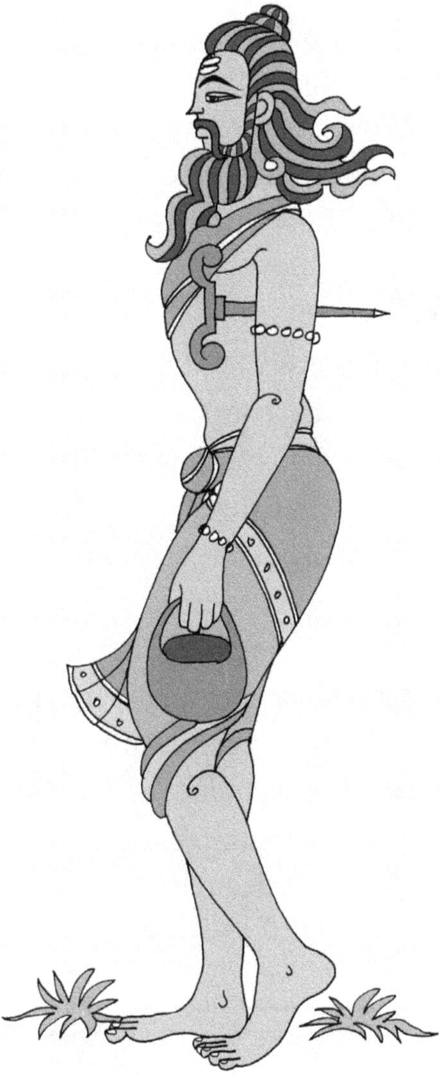

Śatrughna. The four sons understood each other perfectly. Their parents behaved impartially to them. Śrī Rāma was as dear to Kaikēyī as her own life breath.

"It was time for the boys to start their education. In ancient times, there were no schools. The custom was to go to the Guru's home, live there and acquire knowledge from him. Because the four boys were princes, they stayed in the palace and were taught by their family Guru, the venerable Sage Vasiṣṭha. As the first step to learning the Vēdas,[4] the princes underwent the sacred thread ceremony called *Upanayana*. They then learnt the Vēdas and other *śāstras* (sciences) from Vasiṣṭha. They became skilled archers. Śrī Rāma was unrivalled in archery. He would go hunting in the forest to kill the feriocious animals that threatened the life and safety of the citizenry, bring them back and lay them at his father's feet.

"Even though He was a divine incarnation, Śrī Rāma's daily routine set a perfect example for the subjects. He would wake up early in the morning, bathe, chant his mantras, perform his archana,[5] and then touch his parents' feet as a mark of loving respect. He also learnt the law of the land, both civil and moral, to prepare Himself

4 Most ancient of all scriptures, originating from God, the Vēdas were not composed by any human author but 'revealed' in deep meditation to the ancient seers.
5 Chanting of a litany of divine names.

to be the ruler in the future. His three brothers also became adept in the science of administration.

"The people of Ayōdhyā used to line the streets to watch the young princes when they went out to hunt. Everyone in Ayōdhyā shared the pride and joy of the king and his royal consorts. The kingdom was enveloped in the glow of divinity. Peace and prosperity prevailed in the land.

"It was then that it happened," said Grandma solemnly. "It made the king and his queens sad and afraid."

Uṇṇi was startled. "What, Grandma?" he asked anxiously. "What happened?"

"Wait, Uṇṇi. Let me finish," said Grandma. "There was another sage called Viśvāmitra, as learned and revered as Sage Vasiṣṭha. Viśvāmitra was called a *Brahmarṣi,*[6] a title he had earned as a result of long and intense spiritual austerities. King Daśaratha received him with great honour and respect. The king enquired, 'O great sage, to what do we owe the honour of your visit?'

"Viśvāmitra knew of the birth of Lord Rāma and of the reasons behind it. His heart was bursting with the desire to see the young prince. He also wanted to accomplish a few other things. 'I need a small favour,' said Viśvāmitra. The king whole-heartedly agreed to render any help the sage needed.

6 Most exalted of sages.

"'Every month, I conduct a Vēdic ritual to propitiate the gods and our forefathers, but it is regularly disturbed by the demons Mārīca and Subāhu. Please send the princes Rāma and Lakṣmaṇa to kill the demons and protect the yajña. All good will come to you, O great and merciful king,' said the sage.

"The king stood still, too stunned to respond. His darling children had been born after long years of prayers and anguish. How could he send them to face the fierce demons? His two young children would surely be no match for their demonic wiles.

"And yet, Daśaratha could not deny the sage his request either as he had already given him his word. As he stood vexed, unable to decide what to do, he sought the advice of Guru Vasiṣṭha. 'What should I do? I would rather die than let Rāma leave my sight!'

"Vasiṣṭha comforted the distraught father, 'Let me share a great secret with you. Prince Rāma is not an ordinary mortal but an incarnation of God. Lord Viṣṇu Himself has been born to Kausalyā and your royal highness.'"

Uṇṇi's face was shining with joy. He said, "Wow, what an exciting story!"

Grandma smiled. "Vasiṣṭha said, 'O King, in your last birth, you were known as Kaśyapa Prajāpati. Kausalyā, your chief consort, was named Aditi. Both of you prayed earnestly for Lord Viṣṇu to be born as your son. Your prayers have been answered in this birth. Lord Viṣṇu has been born to you as Prince Rāma. The Lord's serpent, Ananta, is Prince Lakṣmaṇa. The Lord's conch and *Sudarśana Cakra* (discus) have been reborn as Bharata and Śatrughna. Have no fear. Send Rāma and Lakṣmaṇa with Sage Viśvāmitra.'

"Daśaratha was greatly relieved. He agreed to send Rāma and Lakṣmaṇa along with the sage."

Grandma caressed Uṇṇi, who had cuddled close to her. "Uṇṇi, the *Rāmāyaṇa* is a play written and directed by the Lord Himself; so, too, our life. Even if we hesitate, the Lord will see to it that we play our part with sincerity."

“ ***The rulers of a country must lead the fight against crime and injustice. Attachment towards their family, thoughts of impending danger, laziness and selfishness should not make them turn a blind eye to the sorrow and suffering of their subjects. Capable officers must be appointed to allay the concerns of the people and to ensure that they live in peace and prosperity.***

5. Killing of Tāṭakā

Today, Uṇṇi's mother, Māḷu, also joined her son to listen to Grandma narrating the stories of Prince Rāma of Ayōdhyā. She told her mother, "Amma, I don't have the time to read the *Rāmāyaṇa*. So, I thought of listening to your narration and enjoying it with Uṇṇi. I have tidied up the house and finished my cooking. Now, I can relax and sit beside the two of you." She hugged Uṇṇi.

Grandma said, "Very good, daughter. It is always good to listen to the stories of the gods."

She began. "Viśvāmitra set off from the palace with Rāma and Lakṣmaṇa. The young princes walked beside the sage, equipped with a quiver full of arrows on their backs and sturdy bows in their hands. After walking a long distance, Viśvāmitra said, 'O Rāma! O Lakṣmaṇa! You have never known hunger and thirst, but we must travel far. I shall initiate both of you into two divine mantras: *bala* and *atibala*. Chanting these mantras will appease your hunger and thirst, and make you strong.'"

"The young princes kept hunger and thirst at bay with the help of the two divine mantras. They crossed River Gangā and entered a thick, dark forest. Viśvāmitra warned the two of them, 'This forest is known as Tāṭakāvanam, because it is home to a fierce demoness named Tāṭakā. She can change her form at will. Nobody travels through this forest because she attacks and kills all travellers. Therefore, Rāmacandra, kill this demoness! No harm will befall You as a result of doing so.'

"Śrī Rāma softly twanged His bow. In answer to His challenge, Tāṭakā appeared roaring in front of them, her huge mouth gaping wide, revealing sharp teeth ready to chomp the princes to pieces. She changed shapes repeatedly, trying to scare the brave princes. She hurled huge rocks and trees at them. Aiming carefully, Rāma let loose an arrow. It found its mark, and the fierce demoness fell dead, her huge form crashing down like a mountain to the ground. From Tāṭakā's dead body emanated a lovely *yakṣī*, a heavenly being. She had been cursed to be born as a demoness. Rāma had liberated her. With great joy and reverence, she prostrated at Śrī Rāma's feet, and left for her heavenly abode."

Uṇṇi smiled in happiness. He felt immensely proud of Rāma's valour and compassion.

"Viśvāmitra was also very pleased with the bravery and calmness that the two princes had demonstrated. He taught them how to use different divine weapons. They stayed overnight at Kāmāśram, and left for Siddhāśram the next day. These āśrams were the abode of forest-dwelling sages."

Grandma paused, "Uṇṇi, do you understand the story? I'm making it very simple for my darling grandson."

Uṇṇi nodded solemnly. "Grandma, as you were narrating the story, I was walking with Śrī Rāma and Lakṣmaṇa in the dark forest."

Grandma looked deeply into her grandson's eyes. "Very good," she murmured softly.

Uṇṇi's mother asked, "Amma, Siddhāśram is Viśvāmitra's āśram, isn't it?"

"Yes, daughter. When they reached there, all the sages came up to them and greeted them with love and humility."

"Viśvāmitra explained to the young princes, 'Rāma and Lakṣmaṇa, this is where I conduct the yajña. As soon as I start, the rākṣasas come flying through the skies, and shower blood, meat and offal into the sacred fire. Thus they defile the altar and its surroundings, forcing us to abandon the yajña. You must destroy the rākṣasas and ensure the continuity of the yajña.'

"Śrī Rāma replied, 'Show us the trouble-makers. My arrows won't miss their mark.'

"Viśvāmitra finished preparations for the yajña. The fire blazed up in the *hōma-kuṇḍa*, the sacrificial fire-pit. At once, the sky became dark with hordes of rākṣasas. A shower of blood started pouring down into the hōma-kuṇḍa and its surroundings.

"Subāhu and Mārīca, the sons of Tāṭakā, were the leaders of the rākṣasas. Śrī Rāma let fly two arrows. One of them pierced the chest of Subāhu, who fell dead to the ground. Mārīca fled the scene, but the arrow unerr-ingly followed him as he rushed to the ocean. Terrified, Mārīca screamed, "Save me! Save me!" and finally took refuge in Śrī Rāma. The compassionate prince pardoned the rākṣasa and called back the arrow. From that day onwards, Mārīca became a true devotee of Lord Rāma.

"The other rākṣasas were killed by Lakṣmaṇa's arrows. Thus the yajña came to a successful conclusion. From the high heavens, the grateful gods and other celestial beings showered flower petals on the earth, especially on the two valiant princes. The heavenly host sang hymns in praise of Rāma and Lakṣmaṇa. Viśvāmitra was beside himself with joy. He hugged the two noble princes, fed them tasty delicacies, and regaled them with stories from the *Purāṇas*.

"On the fourth day, after a good rest, Viśvāmitra said, 'We must not lose any more time. We must travel to the kingdom of Vidarbha, where King Janaka is holding a great yajña. In his palace, there is a special bow called the Tryambaka. We must all go and take a look at this bow.'

"The sage, together with Rāma and Lakṣmaṇa, then left for Vidarbha."

We must not waste time through idleness. We must complete all our work in time. Time gone can never be regained. Time is of great value.

6. Liberation of Ahalyā

Uṇṇi, his mother and grandmother were sitting in the *pūjā* room (room of worship). Uṇṇi clambered onto Grandma's lap, settling down to hear the adventures of the brave princes of Ayōdhyā.

Grandma said, "Viśvāmitra, Rāma and Lakṣmaṇa trekked for many days until they reached Sage Gautama's āśram by the banks of the Gangā. The beauty of the place fascinated the two boys. Trees heavily laden with fruit, flowering shrubs and hanging vines made the hermitage a place of ethereal beauty. And yet the place appeared to be deserted. Rāma and Lakṣmaṇa could see no birds, animals or humans around the hermitage. Śrī Rāma asked 'Who lives in this hermitage?'

"Viśvāmitra answered, 'This is the Sage Gautama's hermitage. For many years, the great ascetic lived here happily with his wife Ahalyā, a devoted wife and woman of ravishing beauty. Gautama was pleased with her loving care. Dēvēndra (also known as Indra), the chief of the gods, once saw Ahalyā and was instantly captivated by her beauty. He wanted to make Ahalyā his own. Dēvēndra could change form at will. Changing his form to that of Sage Gautama, he crept near the hut and crowed like a cock to herald the dawn. Gautama got up, thinking it was almost dawn, and went down to bathe in the Gangā. Taking this opportunity, Dēvēndra entered the Parṇaśāla, the hut of the sage and his wife. Ahalyā thought the sage had returned and welcomed him back.

"In the meantime, when he reached the banks of the Gangā, Gautama realized that sunrise was still hours away, and so hastened back to the āśram. What did he see when he returned?"

"What, Grandma?" Uṇṇi asked with bated breath.

"He saw Dēvēndra and Ahalyā lost in each other. Dēvēndra, sensing danger, fell at Gautama's feet and begged forgiveness, for he knew that the sage had the power to reduce him to ashes. Gautama, blazing with anger, cursed both Dēvēndra and Ahalyā. He cursed that Dēvēndra would become the laughing stock of the whole world. He then cursed Ahalyā, who had seen through Dēvēndra's disguise and yet accepted him: 'May you become a stone, exposed to heat and cold, the rain and sun.'

"Ahalyā begged for liberation from the curse. The sage's heart softened a little. He said, 'Remain here, constantly chanting the name of Rāma with great devotion. Not a single creature will come near this place. After many centuries, the sons of King Daśaratha, Rāma and Lakṣmaṇa, will come this way. When the feet of Rāma, who is an incarnation of Lord Viṣṇu, touches you, you will regain your purity and beautiful form. I shall then welcome you back into my life.'

"Viśvāmitra pointed out to Rāma a stone lying in the front of the hut. He said, 'Rāma, this stone is Ahalyā, who has been absorbed in great meditation, constantly chanting the mighty name of Rāma for many centuries. Release her from the curse by the touch of Your holy feet.'

"Śrī Rāma gently placed His foot on the stone. The stone instantly vanished and the beautiful Ahalyā stood before Him with palms joined in devotion. Rāma gently reassured her, 'I am Rāma.' Ahalyā was lost in rapturous bliss. She had been patiently waiting for the Lord, performing severe penance and devoutly chanting His name. A hymn in praise of Śrī Rāma arose from her heart and she blissfully sang the praises of the young prince. Ahalyā sang of the Lord's glory and His divine attributes, and of the principles leading to His birth. We should all read the song Ahalyā composed in praise of Lord Rāma. It is truly a great hymn.

"Gautama then arrived at the hermitage, and Ahalyā was reconciled with him.

"Uṇṇi," said Grandma, "When you grow up, you must read this hymn of Ahalyā. Will you do that?"

Uṇṇi nodded his head. His mother asked, "Even if we commit great mistakes, if we have sincere devotion and truly repent, God will appear before us, won't He?"

Grandma smiled lovingly at her daughter and said, "Yes, He certainly will."

“ ***Devotion is an inner light. The light of devotion guides us to God.***

7. Sītā's Svayamvara

Grandma lit the oil lamp. Uṇṇi and Māḷu waited expectantly. Grandma looked at their faces gleaming in the light of the lamp. Uṇṇi asked her, "Rāma and Lakṣmaṇa are going to Mithilāpuri with Sage Viśvāmitra, aren't they? They must have started out from Gautamāśram after Rāma liberated Ahalyā."

Grandma said, "Yes, Viśvāmitra insisted that they had no more time to waste, and the three of them set out for Mithilāpuri. The sage knew that the time had come for Rāma to fulfil the reasons for His incarnation. They crossed Gangā and reached Mithilāpuri. King Janaka, who had heard about their arrival, personally escorted them to his palace. He was very happy to see his guests — the two princes and the venerable sage — and he greeted them warmly. He looked at the two princes, glowing like the sun and moon respectively, and asked Sage Viśvāmitra, 'Who are these two boys? Their faces are luminous. They verily look like Nara-nārāyaṇa.'[7] King Janaka, a *rājarṣi* (royal saint), was able to discern the divine nature of the two brothers.

"Viśvāmitra replied, 'They are the sons of the brave king, Daśaratha. This is Rāma, the eldest son, and this is Lakṣmaṇa, the third born. I brought them along to Siddhāśram to protect the holy yajña from the rākṣasas, and if necessary, to kill them. On the way, the demoness

7 Combination of the human (nara) and the Supreme (Nārāyaṇa); the twin brother incarnation of Lord Viṣṇu.

Tāṭakā tried to attack them. Rāma finished her off with a single arrow. The other demons, who tried to defile my yajña, were also killed by the unerring aim of the arrows released by the two princes. Thus they protected the yajña. On the way here, Śrī Rāma liberated Ahalyā, who had been turned into a stone by Sage Gautama's fierce curse. They have come here to see the magnificent Tryambaka, Lord Paramēśvara's renowned bow.'

"King Janaka had four daughters. Sītā was the eldest. However, She was not Janaka's biological offspring. She was found in a furrow of a field being ploughed for a yajña. A girl of extraordinary beauty and divinity, She was named Sītā. King Janaka had brought Her up as if She were his own daughter.

"Now, let me tell you the secret behind Sītā's birth. She was, in reality, Lakṣmi Dēvī, who had incarnated to wed Lord Rāma and to help Him fulfil the reason for his manifestation on earth. Sītā's beauty was beyond description. Her nature was pure and courageous. She spread happiness all around Her by Her mere presence. Sītā was well versed in the scriptures and learnt many skills under her Guru. Her younger sisters, born to Janaka, were Urmiḷā, Māṇḍavī and Śrutakīrti.

"In order to find a groom worthy enough of his beloved Sītā, King Janaka had organized a competition. He declared that he would offer Sītā's hand to the prince who could lift the huge Tryambaka and string it. Many princes tried, but failed to move the huge and heavy bow even an inch. King Janaka knew that the right prince, who would prove worthy of Sītā, would come. When Viśvāmitra requested King Janaka to show the young princes the mighty bow, Janaka secretly thought, 'If only Rāma would string the bow...' The king ordered his minister to bring the bow without any delay. It took nearly 5,000 people to raise the heavy bow and bring it for the princes to see. Śrī Rāma prostrated to the bow. Then, turning to Viśvāmitra, He humbly asked, 'May I lift the bow? And string it?'"

"Uṇṇi's eyes had become big and round. He was breathing hard. Grandma sensed that he was there in the kingdom of Mithilā, along with his heroes, the two young princes of Ayōdhyā.

"Viśvāmitra replied, 'O Rāma, You may do as You wish!'

"With a smile on His lips, the young prince approached the mighty bow of Lord Śiva and effortlessly lifted the Tryambaka. When He strung it, the bow snapped because of the sheer force. The sound of the breaking bow resounded in all the 14 worlds. People stood transfixed. The gods and celestial nymphs showered flowers on the scene from their heavenly abode. The princes who had tried and failed to nudge the divine bow shuddered in fear and astonishment. King Janaka, beside himself with joy, embraced Śrī Rāma.

"Sītā's heart brimmed over with joy. Her attendants dressed Her in wedding finery. Clad in silk robes and wearing exquisite ornaments, Sītā came near Śrī Rāma, holding the wedding garland in Her hands. She came near the prince, smiled shyly and garlanded Him. The land of Mithilā was swept by waves of joy."

Uṇṇi sighed deeply. As he slowly emerged from his reverie, he said, "How wonderful it is, Grandma, to hear Rāma's story."

Māḷu, Uṇṇi's mother, said, "It is not enough to hear the stories, Uṇṇi. You must assimilate the great truths embedded in the *Rāmāyaṇa*."

> ***King Janaka's humility and loving behaviour towards his guests are to be emulated. Śrī Rāma asked for Viśvāmitra's permission and waited patiently for the sage to give his consent before lifting the Tryambaka, even though He knew that He could string the bow with effortless ease.***

8. Śrī Rāma's Humility

Grandma entered the pūjā room and lit the oil lamp. She called her grandson, "Uṇṇi, come! Ask your mother to come also. I'm waiting in the pūjā room."

Mother and son entered the pūjā room.

"Grandma, you were describing the Sītā *Svayamvara*,"[8] Uṇṇi reminded his grandmother.

"I remember well, Uṇṇi. Meditate on Śrī Rāma and listen to the rest of the story."

Grandma continued, "King Janaka was extremely pleased that a valiant prince had come to wed his daughter Sītā. He requested Sage Viśvāmitra to convey the news to King Daśaratha without delay.

"Both of them sat down and composed a letter describing the events of the day, and sent it through royal messengers to Ayōdhyā. On receiving the glad tidings, King Daśaratha set out for Ayōdhyā with his wives, his sons Śatrughna and Bharata, and his Guru Vasiṣṭha and his wife Arundhati-dēvī. They were preceded by a band of musicians playing ceremonial music.

"Janaka and his Guru Shatānanda were waiting for them. The king greeted them warmly. Rāma and Lakṣmaṇa prostrated before their parents and their Guru and his wife. The brothers exchanged news amongst themselves and expressed happiness at the reunion.

8 Practice of choosing a husband from among an array of suitors.

"King Janaka said to King Daśaratha, 'I have four daughters, and you have four sons. I would be honoured if you would agree to marry the four princes to my four daughters.'

"Daśaratha was in total agreement. An auspicious date for the four weddings was fixed by sages Vasiṣṭha, Viśvāmitra and Shatānanda. On that beautiful day, Lord Rāma wedded Sītā, and Lakṣmaṇa married Urmiḷā. Māṇḍavī became the bride of Bharata, and Śrutakīrti married Śatrughna. The wedding celebrations lasted for many days. King Janaka gifted his daughters silken clothes, golden pots, and ornaments studded with precious gems and pearls. He presented Śrī Rāma with elephants, horses, servants, soldiers, chariots and a large coffer of gems.

"When the festivities came to an end, Daśaratha asked for permission to leave, and bade farewell to King Janaka and his wife. He set out on his journey back to Ayōdhyā with his wives, his princes and their brides, to the accompaniment of joyous music. The atmosphere was permeated by the fragrance of sandalwood and musk, and saffron sprays lent a rosy hue to the air. Everyone was in a blissful mood as they wended their way back to the land of Ayōdhyā."

Grandmother lowered her voice and said, "And then it happened."

Uṇṇi's eyes were as wide as saucers. His voice trembled with anxiety as he asked, "What happened to them, Grandma?"

Grandmother said, "Paraśurāma, the scourge of the *kṣatriya* (warrior) race, was standing in the middle of the path, blocking the way of the entourage. He was brandishing His axe menacingly, His mighty bow and arrows slung over His shoulder. His body was quivering with uncontrolled rage. Seeing Paraśurāma approaching them with the fury of a whirlwind, Daśaratha became frightened. What terrible fury! Paraśurāma's face was blazing like the noonday sun. Daśaratha halted before Paraśurāma and, with palms joined together humbly, beseeched Him to spare them from His avenging fury. But there was no abating of Paraśurāma's anger. He said, 'Let me know who other than me answers to the name of Rāma. I hear that He has broken the mighty bow of Śiva and married Princess Sītā. I carry the bow of Viṣṇu. If Rāma has the courage, let Him try to lift it and string it. If He fails to do so, I shall annihilate all of you. Know me to be the merciless enemy of the kṣatriyas.'

"Śrī Rāma remained calm and composed. He addressed the furious Paraśurāma, 'O compassionate one, I am only a boy. How can I confront You in battle? I am neither adept in warfare nor skilled in archery. Nevertheless, as You will destroy us if I turn down Your challenge,

I shall attempt to string Viṣṇu's bow. Please hand it over to me.'

"Śrī Rāma then accepted the bow from Paraśurāma. Do you know what happened next, Uṇṇi? With the ease of picking up a flower and tossing it aside, Śrī Rāma picked up the bow and strung it.

"Paraśurāma realized that Śrī Rāma was an incarnation of Lord Viṣṇu. He circumambulated the young prince with great devotion and sang a hymn in His praise. He then left for the Mahēndra mountains to perform intense penance. Daśaratha and his entourage continued on their way to Ayōdhyā.

"Uṇṇi, when you grow up, you must read the beautiful hymn that Paraśurāma sang in praise of Śrī Rāma. Will you, my dearest grandchild?"

Uṇṇi solemnly nodded his head.

> ***Even if we are intelligent and hold high positions, we must not become proud. Pride comes before a fall. True victory in life is not wealth or position but humility and gentle behaviour. Look at the humble and gentle behaviour of Śrī Rāma.***

9. Coronation of Śrī Rāma

Today, Uṇṇi and his mother were waiting for Grandma inside the pūjā room. Grandma came, fresh from her bath, and sat beside her daughter and grandson. Māḷu lit the oil lamp.

Grandma continued with the story of Śrī Rāma. "King Daśaratha was happy that his four sons had married four beautiful princesses with high morals and pleasing behaviour. Not only the king, the people and even the land of Ayōdhyā rejoiced at their good fortune. Ayōdhyā resembled heaven. The king loved all four of his sons, but he had utmost love for Śrī Rāma, his crown prince. Daśaratha could not tear himself away from Rāma for even a single day. He could not even bear to think of separation from Rāma. He loved and respected all three of his wives, but was most fond of the beautiful Kaikēyī.

"It so happened that Kaikēyī's brother requested princes Bharata and Śatrughna to spend some time with him in the land of Kaikēya. Daśaratha agreed, and the two princes left for Kaikēya. Rāma and Lakṣmaṇa stayed back in Ayōdhyā. It was then that a thought arose in the mind of King Daśaratha. He wanted to crown Prince Rāma, and hand over the reins of the kingdom to him. He summoned Sage Vasiṣṭha and said, 'O Guru, I am getting old. Therefore, I wish to crown Rāma as king without any further delay. My mind is insisting that he should be crowned king at the earliest and most auspicious moment.'

"The king continued, 'Śrī Rāma is beloved by all in Ayōdhyā. I have only one regret. Bharata and Śatrughna are not here, as they have gone at the behest of my brother-in-law to visit his kingdom. Nevertheless, let us not wait. Let us proceed with the coronation ceremony.'

"Guru Vasiṣṭha said, 'In that case, the most auspicious time for the ceremony is tomorrow morning.'

"'Let us crown Rāma king tomorrow then!' decided the king. He ordered the necessary arrangements for the coronation to be made at once. Acting upon Guru Vasiṣṭha's instructions, the Chief Minister Sumantra supervised all the elaborate arrangements. Shall I tell you what the preparations were, Uṇṇi? Elephants with gilded tusks; gaily decorated banners; musical processions; a thousand golden pots filled with sacred water and covered with sandalwood leaves; precious necklaces; beautiful women bearing lit lamps to welcome the prince; on and on went the preparations. The land had a festive air. People were happy and excited. The coronation was going to be a grand festival. After overseeing the preparations for the coronation, Sage Vasiṣṭha walked over to the young prince's palace to inform him about his ascension to the throne the next day.

"Rāma washed the sage's feet with sacred water and sprinkled it on His own head. As he informed the young prince about the coronation, the sage also revealed to Him that Brahmā, Creator of the universe, had told him that Śrī Rāma was the incarnation of Lord Viṣṇu. The sage reminded Śrī Rāma about the secret of His birth. Upon his departure, Rāma shared the news of his impending coronation with Lakṣmaṇa. Lakṣmaṇa was overjoyed."

Grandmother stopped and looked at Uṇṇi, "Uṇṇi, are you listening carefully? Are you following the story?"

"Yes, I am. Please continue, Grandma."

"A courtier, who had listened to Daśaratha and Vasiṣṭha discussing the coronation, ran to Kausalyā with the good news. Kausalyā immediately prayed to Goddess Lakṣmī, to guide her son. While the preparations were being made, Sage Nārada came secretly and met Śrī Rāma. He said, 'Rāma, King Daśaratha has decided to crown You king. I have come here to remind You of the secret mission behind Your incarnation. You were born to destroy the evil rākṣasa Rāvaṇa and his henchmen. Although I am aware that You are all knowing, nevertheless, I have come to remind You once more of your divine mission.'

"Śrī Rāma calmly said, 'O sage. I have neither forgotten my mission nor will I ever break my word. But there is a right time for everything. I am waiting for the opportune time. It has arrived. I will set out from Ayōdhyā tomorrow itself to fulfil my purpose.'

"A happy and relieved Nārada left the palace and returned to the land of the gods. No one else in Ayōdhyā knew that such a conversation had taken place."

> ***There is a time and place for everything. One must wait for the right time. Even an incarnation of God waits for the right moment before acting.***

10. Cunning of Mantharā

Uṇṇi asked his grandmother, "What happened then, Grandma? Was Śrī Rāma crowned King of Ayōdhyā?"

Grandma said, "Don't rush me, Uṇṇi. Listen patiently as I continue with the story of the great Prince Rāma."

Uṇṇi smiled and nodded his head.

"The people of Ayōdhyā were beside themselves with joy. They loved Rāma and wanted him to be crowned king. Flowers were strewn on the royal pathways. Their fragrance wafted about in the air. Colourful banners were hung from the balconies of homes. A steady stream of people from the neighbouring kingdoms started flowing in to Ayōdhyā to witness the grand coronation.

"Mantharā was a hunchback maid of Queen Kaikēyī. She had been with Kaikēyī right from the queen's childhood. She had heard that Śrī Rāma was going to be crowned king the next morning. The news agitated Mantharā. Her face darkened and her heart was filled with cruel thoughts. She walked purposefully towards Kaikēyī's palace.

"Through the palace windows, Kaikēyī was watching the preparations going on in the streets outside. She turned to face Mantharā when the hunchback maid entered her room. 'Mantharā, what's going on? Why's the city being so brightly decorated?'

"With great spite and scorn, Mantharā said, 'Foolish creature, you spend your days in ignorance. You are in grave danger. The king has decided to crown Rāma. What you see are the preparations for the event.'

"Kaikēyī was thrilled! She took off a golden necklace she was wearing and offered it to Mantharā as reward for bringing such auspicious news. 'This news brings me great joy! What is there to be upset about? Rāma is dearer to me than Bharata, and I am dearer to Rāma than his own mother, Kausalyā. I love and trust Rāma. Foolish Mantharā, why do you think that I will be in any danger?'

"A resolve arose in Mantharā's wilful mind to pervert Kaikēyī's attitude towards Śrī Rāma. She said, 'You poor fool! You don't realize that the king is betraying you. Did anybody inform you about the coronation tomorrow? Kausalyā and Sumitrā have already been informed. They have started their celebrations. Sending Śatrughna and Bharata to Kaikēya was a trick the king played so as to hold the coronation ceremony in their absence. When Rāma becomes king, Kausalyā will become queen mother. I wonder what your position will be then! You will probably be made Kausalyā's maid. Bharata will lead the life of a slave. He might be exiled from the kingdom or even executed! Surely, it's better to die than to live as Kausalyā's maid!'

"Fear began to overwhelm Kaikēyī. Doubts arose in her mind. She said, 'I agree with what you're saying. Even if these things happen, what can I do to prevent them?'

"Mantharā said, 'I shall tell you how to handle the situation. Kaikēyī, you are as dear to me as my own life. I am advising you so that you might live happily.' Kaikēyī's mind fell into the trap set by Mantharā. She listened avidly to the wicked maid.

"Mantharā continued, 'Do you remember the battle between the gods and demons? You had accompanied King Daśaratha when he travelled up to heaven. In the middle of the war, the central spoke from one of the wheels of the king's chariot had broken. You had inserted your hand where the broken spoke was and stood there, braving the pain, to protect the king and to allow him to continue fighting. I have always wondered how you bore such unbearable pain for your husband's sake. As a token of his gratitude, the king had promised that he would fulfil two of your desires. You had told the king that you would ask for the boons when the time came. The king had agreed. Don't you remember?'

"'Of course, I remember,' said Kaikēyī. 'But what am I supposed to do now?'

"'Listen Kaikēyī,' said Mantharā, 'Demand that the king fulfils the two boons now. The first boon should be to banish Rāma into the forest for 14 years. For the second boon, demand that Bharata be crowned king. Go at once and lie in the chamber of anger. Remove all your ornaments, wear soiled clothes and lie on the ground. When the king comes in search of you to tell you the news of Rāma's coronation, demand the two boons from him. I am going now.'

"Kaikēyī said, 'I shall remain lying on the floor of the chamber of anger until the king grants me these two wishes. If he does not agree, I shall abandon my body!'

"Mantharā said, 'If you do not waver in your resolve, your demands will definitely be met.' Saying so, she left the palace, jubilant that she had been able to corrupt Kaikēyī's mind."

Māḷu, Uṇṇi's mother, commented, "However good a man may be, if he gets into bad company, there will come a time when everyone will revile him. Am I not right, mother? Kaikēyī became as low and scheming as Mantharā."

Grandma said, "You're right, Māḷu, but we cannot blame anybody in this instance. Mantharā had to say these words so that Śrī Rāma could fulfil the reason for His incarnation. She was just a tool in God's hands."

> ***However good he may be, a man will lose all his goodness if he keeps evil company. We must always be aware and guard ourselves against bad influences.***

11. Boons Granted to Kaikēyī

Grandma, Māḷu and Uṇṇi entered the pūjā room. Uṇṇi said, "You were saying that Kaikēyī was going into the chamber of anger. What's that, Grandma?"

Grandma replied, "It is a room that one goes to when one is furious about something. Kaikēyī entered the room so that others in the palace would know she was angry. She flung away her costly ornaments, rolled on the floor, and dirtied her clothes. Cupping her face in her hands, she started weeping. Her face became stained with the *khol* and the red *sindūr*.

"In the meantime, Daśaratha, who had informed his council of ministers about Rāma's coronation, entered the queens' palace to share the good news with them. As he was fondest of Kaikēyī, he went to see her first. He searched everywhere for her but could not find her. This was puzzling as she was always there to receive him lovingly when he entered her palace. Where could she be?

"He asked Kaikēyī's maids, who told him, 'O king, our mistress has entered the chamber of anger, but we don't know why. Please go there to find out why she's angry.'

"Daśaratha walked quickly into the chamber. He saw a distraught Kaikēyī, rolling on the ground and wailing loudly. Her hair was undone, and her clothes, unkempt. Alarmed by this sight, Daśaratha sat near her on the floor and asked his beloved, "Kaikēyī, what happened? Why are you so sad and upset? Who caused you such distress? Whoever it is, I am ready to kill him or her. Tell me what you want, and I shall see to it that your wish is fulfilled.' He added, 'I swear in the name of Śrī Rāma, who is dearer to me than my own life, that I will grant you what you desire.'

"Hearing this, Kaikēyī sat up. She knew that the king would always honour his word. She said, 'I know that you are always true to your word. So, hear me out. Long ago, I saved your life in the battlefield by stopping your chariot from collapsing in the middle of the battle between the gods and demons. I hope you haven't forgotten about the two boons you promised me that day. Today, I want you to redeem those two boons. Firstly, you must crown Bharata King of Ayōdhyā. Secondly, you must banish Śrī Rāma into the forest for 14 years. If you do not honour these two wishes, be certain that I will end my life!'

"On hearing those words, Daśaratha fainted and fell to the floor. He regained consciousness intermittently, and whenever he did, he would cry piteously. After some time, he looked at Kaikēyī with fear, as if he was in the presence of a cruel tigress. In grief-stricken tones, he asked, 'What happened to you, Kaikēyī? What has Rāma done to you? How did He incur your wrath? Is He not dearest to you? Why do you utter such cruel words?'

"Daśaratha added, 'I shall crown Bharata King of Ayōdhyā. But what need is there to banish Rāma to the forest? Do not fear Him. He will never let any harm come to you. Let Bharata be king. But I beg of you not to ask that Rāma be exiled into the wild forest!'

"Kaikēyī vehemently asked, 'You swore in Śrī Rāma's name to honour your pledge. Will you break your oath? If you do not banish Śrī Rāma to the forest by tomorrow morning, I shall take my life!'

"Daśaratha could not even begin to envisage a separation from his most precious Rāma. He lay on the floor, often losing unconscious, crying out "Rāma! O Rāma, my darling son!' Thus, he spent the whole night lamenting.

"The boons he had once promised Kaikēyī were proving to be his undoing. On the one hand, he was faced with Kaikēyī's stubbornness, and on the other, the heartbreaking thought of sending Śrī Rāma away. Daśaratha felt that he was drowning in a sea of sorrow.

"No one else was aware of these happenings. The subjects were eagerly anticipating the coronation of Śrī Rāma. Vasiṣṭha was overseeing the magnificent preparations. When the palace singers arrived in the morning to sing songs to awaken the king, Kaikēyī stopped them roughly, much to their alarm.

"Young and old, men, women and children were streaming into the capital to witness the historic occasion. They had spent a sleepless night celebrating their favourite prince's impending ascension to the throne. They were longing to see Rāma dressed in kingly robes and adorned with a bejewelled crown. They waited impatiently."

> ***We must think twice before giving our word to anyone, for we must never break our word. Otherwise, quite a few people might have to suffer its consequences. Never make promises on the spur of the moment. Always think deeply before acting.***

12. Stopping of the Coronation

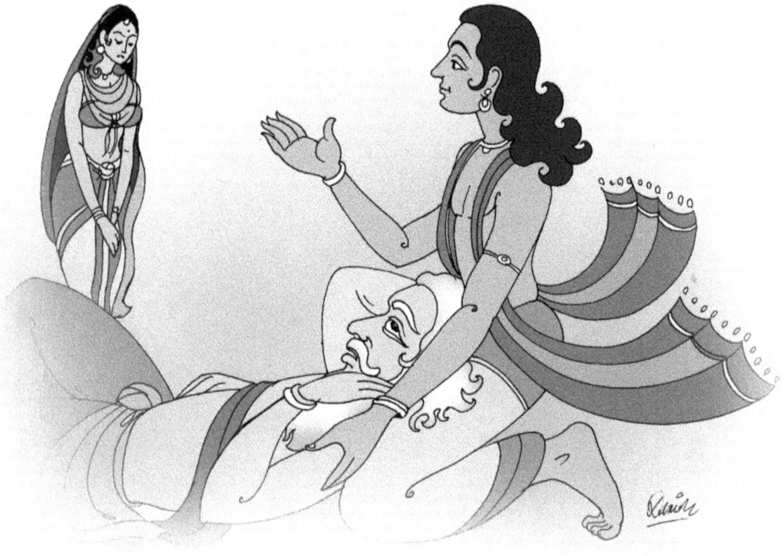

Today, Māḷu reached the pūjā room first and lit the oil lamp. Grandma and Uṇṇi entered after her. Uṇṇi garlanded the pictures of the gods in the pūjā room. There was a picture of Rāma and Lakṣmaṇa wielding bows and arrows. Goddess Sītā was to the left of Rāma. Lying prostrate with love and devotion at His feet was Hanumān. Grandmother gazed at the freshly garlanded picture for a long time. Her eyes filled with tears of devotion.

Grandma said, "Let's continue, Uṇṇi. As he lay on the floor begging Kaikēyī to show mercy, Daśaratha was like a man who had lost his senses. He kept calling out in great anguish, 'Rāma... Rāma... my son...' Not having any inkling of the tragedy unfolding inside, Sumantra came to see the king. The Chief Minister was shocked to see him lying on the ground in that abject state. He asked Kaikēyī, who was standing nonchalantly beside the king, 'O Kaikēyī, why is the king so distraught? Please tell me what happened.'

"Kaikēyī said, "The king could not sleep last night as he was constantly thinking of Rāma and chanting his name. He is distraught because of Rāma. If Rāma comes to him, all his worries will disappear. Therefore, please summon Rāma to His father's presence at once.'

"Sumantra awaited the command from the king, who said, 'Bring my beautiful prince to my side. I want to see him now!' Sumantra went to Rāma and informed Him of the king's condition. Rāma went at once to the palace with Lakṣmaṇa. The sight that greeted the princes was heart-breaking: Daśaratha was lying forlorn on the floor. At the sight of Rāma, he stretched out his hands to his son and called out 'Rāma! Rāma!' before losing consciousness.

"Rāma knelt down and cradled his father's head in his lap. Some of the palace women, suspecting that something was amiss, came running behind the princes. When they saw the king on the floor, they started wailing loudly. Hearing their cries, Vasiṣṭha came to the scene.

"Rāma asked 'Why is my father so upset? Can anyone tell me?'

"It was Kaikēyī who spoke. 'Long ago, your father promised to grant me two boons. He is upset because he does not know how to communicate this to You. Only You can ensure that he does not go back on his word.'

"'Oh, is that all?' asked Śrī Rāma, looking relieved. 'I shall obey any of my father's commands. Don't you know that, as his son, I am duty-bound to honour his word, come what may? O mother, tell me, what do you want me to do? Whatever it is, I give you my word that I shall obey you.'

"Without any hesitation, Kaikēyī told him, "I have demanded two boons from your father: first, that my son Bharata be crowned king with the same sacred materials that have been collected and prepared for Your coronation; second, that You must go and live in the forest in the garb of an ascetic for 14 years.'

"Hearing this, Śrī Rāma asked his father, 'O father? Why did you hesitate to tell me any of this? Let Bharata be crowned king. He is capable of ruling the kingdom. I shall set off for the forest this very moment. O father, do not grieve anymore.'

"Daśaratha said, 'My son, I cannot live without You for even a single moment. Capture me and throw me into the dungeons. You can become the king. No harm will come to you.'

"Rāma said, 'Why do you grieve over this turn of events? I have the strength to give up the kingdom and to live a hermit's life in the forest for 14 years. I shall go and seek the blessings of mother Kausalyā, inform Sītā, and set out at once for the forest.'

"When Śrī Rāma entered Kausalyā's palace, He saw His mother seated in the pūjā room. She was meditating for an auspicious life for her son. Sumitrā roused Kausalyā from her deep meditation and told her of Rāma's arrival. Kausalyā came to greet him and kissed His forehead, 'Why is Your face so pale, Rāma? Are You hungry? Come, let me serve You food.'

"His mother's affection made Rāma sad. Controlling His emotions, He told her, 'No, mother. I have no time to eat with you now. I am going to live in the forest for 14 years. My father has granted two boons to mother

Kaikēyī: that he would crown Bharata king and exile me to the forest for 14 years. I must leave for the forest at once to honour my father's words. You must not worry about me.'

"As Rāma finished speaking, Kausalyā fell unconscious to the ground."

> ***The love that parents have towards their children is immeasurable. Nevertheless, truth and honour must be upheld at any cost, and should not be sacrificed because of affection towards one's own. A word given must be honoured. Śrī Rāma shows us how to face the misfortunes of life calmly. Only unshakeable faith in God will help us make the right decisions without faltering.***

13. Advice to Lakṣmaṇa

Grandmother continued, "When Kausalyā came out of her swoon, she told Rāma, 'Rāma, my son, if You're going to the forest, then I'm coming with You. I cannot live here without You. Let Bharata be king. But why should You be exiled to the forest? Your father has banished You to the forest. As your mother, I am commanding You to stay here. If You disobey me and go to the forest, I shall give up my life!'

"Lakṣmaṇa, who had overheard the conversation between mother and son, could no longer control his anger and grief. Lakṣmaṇa was hot-tempered by nature. In his eyes blazed such anger as would reduce the whole world to ashes. 'Mother Kaikēyī has become mad!' he ranted. 'She has lost her senses. My father is heeding the words of a shameless lunatic. I will not allow him to become a slave to such a woman and to bring disaster upon us. I shall chain him and throw him into the dungeons, and crown my elder brother king.'

"Śrī Rāma embraced his brother, who was seething with rage. He calmed Lakṣmaṇa down with wise words and made him understand the nature of life. We must all read and assimilate the spiritual truths Śrī Rāma imparted to Lakṣmaṇa. At this age, Uṇṇi might not be able to understand Rāma's words. I shall condense it for Māḷu. Uṇṇi, you can also listen to what I'm going to say. When you grow up, you must read and take to heart the advice Rāma gave Lakṣmaṇa."

In a serious voice, Uṇṇi said, "All right, Grandma. But maybe I can understand Rāma's advice even now."

Grandma smiled fondly at her young grandson and hugged him. She said, "I shall try to explain it in simple words."

"Śrī Rāma said, 'Lakṣmaṇa, listen to me. Give up this anger and competitiveness. We live in this world for a very short period of time. We are like wayfarers who meet at a roadside inn, spend some time with each other, and then go our own ways. Nothing in this world is forever. Life is ephemeral, uncertain. The ones who do not know God are not aware of the passage of time. Our body is destined to grow old and die. But we forget this and act with overweening pride. We are enslaved by many desires. You are now under such an illusion. This is why you want to burn the world down. Let go of the pride in your body, and acquire the faith that the supreme self, residing within you, is the only truth.

"'Lakṣmaṇa, knowledge is veiled by desire, anger, greed and longing. Anger is the most powerful veil. One might even kill one's own parents, siblings and friends while in the grip of anger. Therefore, my dear younger brother, control your temper. Anger will destroy goodness and righteousness. Only the Supreme can give you true peace. When such peace dawns, there will be grief no more. Meditate upon the all-pervasive, eternal, infinite and divine consciousness that is witness to all that happens in the world. You have been granted a human life. Your duty is to act without desire and attachment. Offer all your actions to God. Remember God, who is the infinite truth. Give up your pride.'

"After advising Lakṣmaṇa to abandon his anger, Śrī Rāma again turned to his mother, 'Mother, do not grieve. Parting of ways is the very nature of the world. I shall return to you after my 14 years in the forest. Remember your duties to my father. Consider his wishes to be your own. Give me permission to go to the forest with a joyful heart.'

"After speaking these words, Śrī Rāma prostrated at His mother's feet. Kausalyā's mind had become calm and clear. She planted a kiss on the top of Rāma's head. With tears streaming down her face, she prayed, 'O Brahmā, Viṣṇu and Paramaśiva, Protectors of the world, O Goddess Durgā, protect my son as He walks, sits and sleeps.'"

Grandmother continued, "This is a prayer that all parents should have for their children. When Lakṣmaṇa saw that Kausalyā had given Rāma permission to leave, he said, 'Elder brother, I'm coming with You. I shall accompany You throughout your exile. If You do not let me come with You, I will give up my body!'

"Śrī Rāma smiled fondly at his younger brother and said, 'You may come.'"

"We must face whatever happens with calmness and composure. We must hold on to God and do our duties with a clear conscience. Let us dedicate all our actions to God. It is He who rewards us. Doing all work in the spirit of worship will do us immeasurable good.

14. Rāma-Sītā Principles

The oil lamp was lit inside the pūjā room. Grandmother, Māḷu and Uṇṇi prostrated before the deities and sat down in front of the lamp.

"Where did I stop? Do you remember, Uṇṇi?" Grandma asked.

"Yes, Grandma. Lakṣmaṇa wanted to accompany Śrī Rāma into the forest, and Śrī Rāma had agreed," said Uṇṇi.

"Oh yes! Sītā was not at all aware of what was happening in the queens' quarters. Rāma went to Sītā's palace to break the news to Her. Seeing Him, Sītā got up and joyfully washed His feet with water from a golden pot. She asked him, 'Why have you come alone, and that, too, on foot? Where are Your attendants?'

"Śrī Rāma said, "I must leave now for the forest. This is my father's decision. Therefore, do not feel sad about it. Stay with my mother, Queen Kausalyā. I will return after 14 years.'

"Sītā was stunned. She said, 'What are You saying? Your father cannot live without You even for one night. How could he have made such a decision? I don't understand!'

"Śrī Rāma replied, 'A long time ago, father had promised to grant mother Kaikēyī two boons. She asked for those two boons today. One is to crown Bharata King of Ayōdhyā, and the other is to send me away to the forest for 14 years. In order to honour his words, father granted her the two boons. Please do not try to stop me, Sītā. Live happily with my mother, and I will return after 14 years.'

"Sītā replied, 'If You are going to the forest, I shall walk in front of you. You should come after me. A husband and wife should never be parted from each other.'

"Śrī Rāma tried to explain to Sītā the difficulties of forest life: 'The jungle is full of thick trees. There are dangerous wild animals like lions, leopards, wild boars, bison, bears and wolves that roam the forest. There are also rākṣasas that catch and eat humans. You will not get good food. You will not see other human beings. The forest is full of rocks, and the ground will be rough and rocky in many places.'

"But Sītā had already made up Her mind. She firmly said, 'Who else can I depend upon other than You? If I have to walk on rough ground, when You are beside me, I will feel as if the ground is strewn with flowers. When You are with me, fear will not enter my mind.'

"Hearing Her words, Śrī Rāma said, 'In that case, Sītā, You may also come with me.'

"Rāma gave away His clothes, jewellery and cows to the *Brāhmins.*[9] Sītā gifted Arundhati, Guru Vasiṣṭha's wife, many precious objects. Lakṣmaṇa sought permission from his mother Sumitrā to follow Rāma into the forest. He entrusted his mother to the care of Kausalyā. Sumitrā told him, 'My son, always be with your elder

9 Members of the priestly caste.

brother. Take care of all His needs. Consider Śrī Rāma your father and Sītā your mother. Regard the forest as Ayōdhyā. Go and return in peace.'

"Lakṣmaṇa took his mother's words to his heart. He slung his bow and arrows over his shoulder and stood beside Rāma. Rāma, Lakṣmaṇa and Sītā set out to bow down before their father and seek his blessings.

"In the meantime, news of the tragedy had spread like wildfire in the palace and the rest of the kingdom. People learnt about the two boons Kaikēyī had asked for and that Daśaratha had been forced to grant. The people heard that Rāma was being banished to the forest. They talked amongst themselves, 'The king has granted Kaikēyī two boons. Bharata will become king, and Śrī Rāma will be sent to the forest. Why should we live in an Ayōdhyā without Śrī Rāma? Let us all accompany Him to the forest!'

"Vāmadēva Maharṣi, who was a *jñānī* (knower of the Truth), calmed the subjects by telling them the truth about Rāma: 'Do not grieve for Rāma. He is an incarnation of Lord Nārāyaṇa. When love, compassion, truth and justice decline in this world, the Lord incarnates to re-establish *dharma* (righteousness). He has saved the earth through His other incarnations: Matsya, Kūrma, Varāha, Narasimha, Vāmana and Paraśurāma. Now, the time has come to destroy the powerful rākṣasa king Rāvaṇa. Lord Nārāyaṇa has manifested as Śrī Rāma, son of King Daśaratha, for this purpose. Therefore, do not feel upset about the fate of Śrī Rāma, Lakṣmaṇa and Sītā.' Hearing this, people started to calm down."

Grandmother then said, "That's enough for today, Uṇṇi. I shall tell you about their journey to the jungle tomorrow." Uṇṇi heaved a sigh of contentment and hugged his grandmother.

> **"** ***Sumitrā, who did not falter but faced the inevitable with great calm, is an example for all of us. Not only did she allow her son to go on the perilous journey with Śrī Rāma, she also gave him strength and noble advice. We should learn to face all situations with such equipoise.***

15. Journey to the Forest and Meeting with Guha

Grandmother was meditating on the form of Lord Rāma. She opened her eyes as Uṇṇi and Māḷu sat quietly beside her. They listened earnestly as she continued the story of the brave Prince Rāma.

"Rāma, Lakṣmaṇa and Sītā went to the palace of Kaikēyī to bid farewell to their father. Rāma reassured Kaikēyī, 'Mother, do not worry anymore. The three of us are leaving for the forest now.'

"This was what Kaikēyī had been longing to hear. She gave them garments fashioned from tree bark. Śrī Rāma and Lakṣmaṇa took off their princely robes and attired themselves in the bark. Those who were watching could not hide their tears when they saw the noble princes dressed like foresters, with only the bark of trees to clothe them. When Sītā started to put on the tree bark, Sage Vasiṣṭha's heart melted in sorrow. He felt great anger towards Kaikēyī. He said, 'O cruel, stone-hearted woman! How dare you offer Princess Sītā the bark of a tree to wear? The chaste Sītā will wear Her silken robes and golden ornaments as She accompanies Her husband to the forest!'

"Sumantra then brought the chariot. Unable to bear the grief, Daśaratha fell to the ground, crying, 'Rāma, my son!' Without losing his composure, Śrī Rāma bowed down to his father. He then helped Sītā into the chariot and got in after Her. Lakṣmaṇa followed, bearing bows and quivers of arrows in hand.

"As the chariot started to move, Daśaratha cried, 'Stop, my son! Stop!' But Rāma commanded Sumantra to forge ahead. When the chariot disappeared from sight, Daśaratha fell unconscious. Many subjects ran behind the chariot, unable to part with the noble prince.

"Daśaratha's condition was pitiful. He started crying, and incoherent words tumbled out of his mouth. His attendants took the disconsolate king to Kausalyā's quarters. The grieving Daśaratha and Kausalyā were inconsolable.

"By nightfall, Rāma's chariot reached the banks of Tamasā River. Sītā and Rāma drank some water and slept peacefully underneath a tree. Lakṣmaṇa stood watch, and shared his grief and anger with Sumantra, Daśaratha's chief minister. The people of Ayōdhyā also went to sleep by the riverbank.

"Waking up before dawn, Śrī Rāma softly whispered to Sumantra, 'My people are still asleep. They will wake up when the sun rises, and prevent me from going any further. We must leave before they awaken.' They left quietly without waking anybody.

"When the sun rose and the people of Ayōdhyā awoke, they realised that their prince had already entered the dense forest and was lost to them. With sobbing hearts, they turned and made their way back to the capital city.

"Śrī Rāma, Sītā and Lakṣmaṇa reached the banks of the Gangā. They sat under the sheltering branches of the

Śimśapa tree in a place called Śṛngavēra. A forest dweller named Guha was the King of Śṛngavēra and an ardent devotee of Śrī Rāma. When he realized that Śrī Rāma, Sītā and Lakṣmaṇa had reached his kingdom, Guha was overjoyed. He collected the most delicious fruits, wild honey and fragrant flowers, which he humbly offered at Śrī Rāma's feet. Śrī Rāma got up and enfolded Guha in a deep embrace. Guha bowed before Rāma and said, 'My land has become blessed by the touch of Your holy feet. Please accept this kingdom of mine. Remain here and rule over us, your loyal subjects. Sanctify my palace with the dust of Your feet. Please bless me by accepting these fruits and flowers.'

"Śrī Rāma gently and lovingly declined the offer. He told Guha that He would not accept any offering for 14 years, but on his return 14 years later, He would accept Guha's hospitality. He requested the gum of the banyan tree from Guha, mixed holy ash in it, and tied his hair up in a matted knot. Guha spread a mattress of leaves and grass for Sītā and Ram to sleep on. They accepted his loving devotion. Lakṣmaṇa remained awake, watching over his beloved brother and sister-in-law.

"Guha could not stop the tears streaming down his face as he lamented to Lakṣmaṇa, 'How could this happen to Śrī Rāma, who ought to be sleeping on a silken mattress? How could Kaikēyī heed Mantharā's words and commit such a sin?'

"Lakṣmaṇa had taken Śrī Rāma's advice to heart. He told Guha, 'Listen carefully to what I say. All of us reap the fruits of actions we have performed in our previous lives. Sorrow and happiness are the consequences of our own actions. No one else is responsible for our fate. We must learn to accept calmly whatever situations we face. We must neither drown in sorrow when bad things happen nor overly rejoice when good things happen. Joy and sorrow are constant visitors. We must face both with courage and equanimity.'

"They continued talking to each other until dawn broke. Śrī Rāma and Sītā awoke. In accordance with Śrī Rāma's request, Guha brought a boat to take them across the Gangā. They stepped into the boat. Sītā prostrated before Goddess Gangā. Guha ferried them across, and then humbly begged permission to accompany them. Śrī Rāma gently said, "Do not grieve. Return home. I give you my word that I will return after 14 years.' Guha had gathered courage from Lakṣmaṇa's words. He prostrated before Śrī Rāma and returned home."

"Do good. Calmly face the sorrows that visit your life. Do not allow the base emotions of cruelty and revenge to enter your mind. Good actions will reap good rewards. This is most certain.

16. Visits to Bharadvāja's and Vālmīki's Hermitages

Uṇṇi and Māḷu reached the pūjā room before Grandmother. Śrīkuṭṭi was in Māḷu's lap. She was sleeping, a doll clutched in one chubby hand. Grandmother entered the pūjā room and sat silently with closed eyes for a few minutes.

Uṇṇi said, "Grandma, Śrī Rāma bade farewell to Guha, promising to visit him after 14 years. What happened then?"

Grandmother said, "Listen carefully, dear Uṇṇi. Not far from there was the hermitage of Sage Bharadvāja, a great ascetic. Śrī Rāma walked to the āśram with Sītā and Lakṣmaṇa, and sent word of their arrival to the sage through a small boy they met at the edge of the āśram. Bharadvāja was very happy to receive the news. With water and pūjā utensils in his hands, he went to meet and honour Śrī Rāma. He worshipped Śrī Rāma with great devotion and became immersed in bliss. Śrī Rāma and Lakṣmaṇa prostrated to the sage. Bharadvāja took them to his hermitage and said, 'O Rāmacandra, please sanctify my hermitage with the touch of your holy feet. My eye of wisdom has opened only because of my love for and devotion to You, who are the very embodiment of wisdom. With my eye of wisdom, I realized who You are and also divined that You had left Ayōdhyā and travelled to the forest. I also know why You are spending time in the forest. My life has been fulfilled because I have now been blessed by the sight of Your physical form.'

"Śrī Rāma prostrated before the sage and humbly replied, 'Please bless us, who have been born into the *kṣatriya* (warrior) race.'

"The three of them spent the night in the sage's hermitage. The next day, they crossed the Gangā with the help of the sage's sons. At a distance, they saw the hermitage of Sage Vālmīki. Śrī Rāma and Vālmīki lived at the same time."

"I know," said Uṇṇi.

"Vālmīki's hermitage was extremely beautiful, peaceful and grand. It is difficult to describe it. There were many flowering trees and trees laden with fruits. Many animals and birds made their home here. Śrī Rāma, Sītā and Lakṣmaṇa walked up to Vālmīki and prostrated at His feet. On seeing Śrī Rāma, the sage's eyes overflowed with tears. He stood gazing at Rāma, not daring to close His eyes. 'Who is this! Is it not Lord Viṣṇu Himself, consort of Goddess Lakṣmī? He is now standing before me as Śrī Rāma, with matted hair tied in a knot on top of His head, clothed in the bark of a tree, armed with bow and arrows, and blessing me with the sight of His divine form!' Overwhelmed by these thoughts, Vālmīki hugged Śrī Rāma with great love and happiness, and worshipped Him ceremonially. He offered Śrī Rāma, Sītā and Lakṣmaṇa ripe fruits and fresh vegetables. They partook of the food and felt greatly refreshed.

"Rāma told Vālmīki, 'In obedience to my father's command, I set out for the forest in the company of Sītā and Lakṣmaṇa. I know You are an adherent of Vēdānta.[10] I have no need to tell you why I left for the forest as you are farsighted. Please tell us a place where we can stay. The three of us want to spend a few days somewhere near.'

"Vālmīki felt very happy. He said, 'O Rāma, do You need a place to stay? All the worlds reside in You. You abide as bliss in the hearts of divine souls. O Rāma, You, who are the supreme self, please enter the hearts of those who are established in devotion to You, whose hearts are purified by devotion and soaked in love for You. Remain happily in their hearts with Sītā, Your consort.'

"He then told Rāma the story of how He became a sage by chanting the Rāma mantra."

Grandma asked, "Do you remember the story of Ratnākaran, who kept on chanting the Rāma mantra until he was transformed into Sage Vālmīki?"

"Yes, Grandma," said Uṇṇi. "He was chanting the name of Rāma inside an anthill when the sages came and pulled him out."

Grandma continued, "Vālmīki narrated His own story to Śrī Rāma. He said, 'I became what I am today because of the glory and power of Your name. I now have the great fortune of seeing Your divine physical form, accompanied

10 'End of the Vēdas.' It refers to the Upaniṣads, which deal with the subject of Brahman, the Supreme Truth, and the path to realize that Truth.

by Sītā and Lakṣmaṇa. O Rāma! I shall tell You of a place to stay. Build a beautiful āśram between the Citrakūṭa Mountain and the Gangā.'

"Accordingly, the three of them built a beautiful āśram in the forest and lived there in peace and happiness."

> ***We must gain devotion by constantly remembering God. The abode of God is a heart filled with devotion, trust and faith. When God enters our heart, we will become blissful.***

17. Death of Daśaratha

Uṇṇi, Māḷu and Grandma prostrated before the lamp in the pūjā room. The light from the lamp cast a gentle glow on the pictures of the deities.

Grandmother continued the narration of the *Rāmāyaṇa*. "Sītā, Rāma and Lakṣmaṇa built a beautiful āśram for themselves at the foothills of Citrakūṭa Mountain, and lived there in peace and happiness. Now, let us look at what was happening in Ayōdhyā.

"Sumantra, Daśaratha's chief minister, returned to Ayōdhyā, his heart heavy with sadness. He met King Daśaratha, who asked him, 'How are my children? Did they have any message for this great sinner? O God, I will not be blessed to take my last breath in the presence of my sweet children!'

"Sumantra told the king, who was thus berating himself, 'Obeying your order, I drove them in my chariot. As we were resting by the bank of the Gangā near the town of Śṛngavēra, the local ruler, Guha, came and offered his salutations to Śrī Rāma. He brought along fruits and honey. The prince requested tree gum and other materials needed to tie His hair up in a matted knot. As He climbed into Guha's boat, He told me, "Offer my salutations to my father and mothers. Tell father not to

grieve on my behalf." Sītā Dēvī was crying as She said, "Offer my salutations at my mothers' feet." Guha rowed them across the Gangā. I stood and looked at the three of them until they disappeared from sight. I stood there like a corpse. Then I went back to the chariot and came swiftly back to you.'

"Kausalyā, who was standing beside Daśaratha and listening to his lament, spoke. 'You could have handed the kingdom over to Kaikēyī. Why did you have to exile Rāma to the forest? What's the point of lamenting like this now?'

"Daśaratha replied, 'Why do you remind me again and again of my folly, and increase my sorrow?' He then recounted an incident that had happened a long time ago. Once, he had gone hunting and was eager to kill an animal. Reaching a riverbank at midnight, he heard a sound nearby. It was a young hermit filling his pot with water from the river. In the darkness, the king mistook the sound for an elephant drinking water. His arrow unerringly hit the target, mortally wounding the young boy. When the king ran up to him, the boy started weeping, 'Oh, I'm going to die! I have done no harm to anyone, and yet I have been hurt this way. My parents are old and blind. They are very thirsty. Who will give them water now?'

"The king, realizing his grave error, confessed to the boy that he had mistaken the sound of him filling his water-pot for an elephant drinking water. He revealed that he was king of the country. He then fell at the feet of the young sage and begged his pardon. The boy said, 'O King! No harm will come to you. Remove the arrow from my body and relieve my pain. Then go to my aged parents and quench their thirst. Let them know of my fate.'

"Daśaratha pulled the arrow out of the young sage's body, whereupon the boy died. He took the pot of water, went to his old parents, and recounted what had happened. They began wailing in grief. After some time, they requested Daśaratha, 'Please take us to the spot where our son has fallen.'

"Daśaratha took them there. The old couple began their heart-breaking laments while caressing their son's body. On their instructions, the king prepared a funeral pyre for the young boy, placed his body upon the wooden logs, and lit the pyre. As the fire burned brightly, the old parents entered the pyre. As the flames were devouring him, the old man cursed King Daśaratha: 'You will also die grieving for your son!'

"As he finished narrating this incident to Kausalyā, the king told her, 'The time for the fulfilment of the curse has arrived.' He fell to the floor, and his laments filled the air: 'Rāma... Rāma... Rāma... Sītā... Lakṣmaṇa... Śrī Rāma!' Thus, Daśaratha departed from this world."

Daśaratha had always remained steadfast to truth and justice. However, a lapse in discernment led to grave consequences. Do not act until you have been able to judge correctly the merits and demerits of an action.

18. Arrival of Bharata

Uṇṇi asked his Grandmother, "Grandma, when Daśaratha died, none of his four sons were beside him, right? How did Śrī Rāma learn about his father's death?"

Māḷu said, "The curse of the old man really hit the nail on its head."

Grandma said, "The words of sages and ascetics always come true. The whole of Ayōdhyā began mourning the loss of their king. On Vasiṣṭha's instructions, the king's body was placed inside an oil boat."

Uṇṇi asked, "Why did they do that, Grandma?"

"So that the body does not start decomposing. His sons had yet to return. After his body was preserved, a messenger was sent to the land of Kaikēya to bring Bharata and Śatrughna back. When the news was broken to their uncle, Kaikēyī's brother, he immediately made arrangements for the two princes to return to Ayōdhyā. He did not, however, reveal to them the news of their father's death.

"Bharata's and Śatrughna's minds became unsettled. Bharata started imagining the worst, that some danger had befallen his father and two brothers. They rode their horses home swiftly. When they entered Ayōdhyā, they noticed that it was eerily silent and desolate, with no sign of merriment. Fear and sorrow entered Bharata's mind. Even the palace seemed shorn of its vibrant glory.

"As soon as he reached the palace, Bharata rushed to Kaikēyī's quarters. She hugged him joyfully and asked him about the happenings in Kaikēya. Bharata interrupted her and asked, 'Where is my father? He is always with you.'

"Kaikēyī replied, 'Your father has ascended to the heavens, but you need not fear. I have worked everything out for your benefit.'

"Bharata was greatly anguished to hear the news of his father's demise. He asked, 'Mother, what did my father say at the time of his death?'

"'As he took his last breath, the king was lamenting, "Rāma... Rāma... Rāma... Sītā... Lakṣmaṇa... Śrī Rāma!"'

"Puzzled by Kaikēyī's answer, Bharata asked, 'Why? Why did he cry out for them? Wasn't my elder brother beside him?'

"In response to his distraught questions, Kaikēyī told him about the two boons that the king had promised her in the battlefield. She had asked for Śrī Rāma to be banished to the forest for 14 years, and told him that Sītā and Lakṣmaṇa had followed Him. The second boon that she had asked for and received from the king was that Bharata should be crowned King of Ayōdhyā. She said, 'He honoured his promise to make you King of Ayōdhyā. You will now be crowned the ruler! My son has received what he deserves. Rejoice in this.'

"Inflamed by anger, Bharata started yelling at his mother. 'O cruel women! Rākṣasī! Merciless creature! I have become a sinner because I have been born from your womb! I am going to take my own life! You will go to hell for your cruel and base deeds!'

"Unable to bear his anguish, Bharata ran crying to Kausalyā's quarters. She hugged Bharata and said with tears in her eyes, 'I know that it is Nārāyaṇa Himself who has been born as my son. Nevertheless, His fate grieves me.'

"Prostrating before mother Kausalyā, Bharata said, 'O mother, I swear that I have no part in this horrible act! Mother Kaikēyī acted of her own accord to thwart the coronation of Śrī Rāma.'

"Kausalyā consoled him. 'My son, no harm will come to you.' She embraced him once more. Those present could not help crying at this pitiable sight. Sage Vasiṣṭha consoled Bharata and Kausalyā."

Māḷu asked her mother, "How did Sage Vasiṣṭha console Bharata and Kausalyā? How did he give hope to the two of them, lamenting over Daśaratha's death?"

"He offered them the following words of advice: 'The king passed away only after discharging all his royal responsibilities. He had also enjoyed all the privileges and pleasures of the position. This worldly life is insignificant. The eternal truth is the supreme self, the *Paramātma*. This body will perish but the Self dwelling within the body is imperishable. It is not born; nor does it die. The Self in the king now dwells in his heavenly abode, along with the *dēvas* (gods). Therefore, calm your mind, control your sorrow, and make preparations for the cremation of the king's body.'

"Bharata performed all the prescribed rituals, as instructed by Vasiṣṭha. As part of the rituals, he donated cows, villages, jewels and clothes to Brāhmins. Even while doing so, he was absorbed in thoughts of Śrī Rāma. Vasiṣṭha summoned Bharata and Śatrughna to the palace court. In the presence of the ministers and select citizens of Ayōdhyā, he announced, 'O Bharata! This land of Ayōdhyā has been given to you in order to honour King Daśaratha's word to Kaikēyī. Therefore, we have decided to crown you King of Ayōdhyā without further delay. May all good come to you!'"

> ***Those who understand right and wrong will not be swayed by personal attachment. Bharata did not try to justify Kaikēyī's unjust act. Even the bond between mother and son is subservient to dharma, the code of moral conduct.***

19. Bharata's Journey to the Forest

Grandmother continued, "Bharata responded to his Guru with utmost respect. 'You have told me to accept kingship in deference to my father's order. But what need have I for this land? My elder brother is the rightful heir to the throne of Ayōdhyā. I shall set out early tomorrow morning to bring him back here. I would like all the eminent citizens of Ayōdhyā, ministers, courtiers, palace residents, you and your wife to accompany me. Let the musicians come along to celebrate the return of my elder brother to this land. Until Rāma returns to Ayōdhyā, Śatrughna and I will not accept the comforts of life. For clothing, we shall wear the bark of trees, and tie our hair in matted knots. We shall sleep on the floor, and eat only fruits and tubers.'

"Early the next morning, Sage Vasiṣṭha, his wife, Daśaratha's three queens, ministers and the distinguished citizens, along with the army, accompanied Bharata as he went in search of Śrī Rāma. When they reached Śṛngavēra, Guha mistook their arrival as a challenge to Śrī Rāma, and made hasty preparations to defend his Lord. But when he noticed Bharata dressed in the bark of a tree, wearing his hair matted in a topknot, and uttering 'Rāma... Rāma... Rāma...' with intense devotion and pain, he greeted them reverentially. Guha took Bharata to the tree under which Rāma and Sītā had slept, and near which Lakṣmaṇa had kept armed vigil all night long.

"Bharata asked, 'Where is my brother now?'

"Guha replied, 'As you cross the river Gangā, you will see the Citrakūṭa Mountains. Rāma, Lakṣmaṇa and Sītā are living there in peace and happiness.'

"Bharata said, 'Please help us cross the Gangā.'

"Guha arranged 500 boats to ferry the huge contingent across the Gangā. In the biggest boat sat Guru Vasiṣṭha and his wife, along with Kausalyā, Kaikēyī and Sumitrā. Bharata and Śatrughna climbed in last. Guha himself rowed them across. In this manner, 500 fully loaded boats reached the other side of the river.

"Bharata and Śatrughna trekked to Sage Bharadvāja's āśram and prostrated before Him. Bharata was aware that the sage was a seer who knew past, present and future. Nevertheless, he disclosed why he had come wearing the garb of bark and matted hair in a topknot. 'I have come to find my brother Śrī Rāma, crown Him King of Ayōdhyā, and take Him back with me to rule over the land.'

"Hearing this, the sage enfolded the prince in a deep embrace. He treated all his guests to a sumptuous feast and arranged space for them to rest and sleep."

Uṇṇi asked, "How could the sage arrange food for so many people?"

Grandma laughed, pleased at the question. "Uṇṇi, that was a miracle. The sage had a cow named Kāmadhēnu, who could fulfil every wish of her owner. Sage Bharadvāja entered his meditation room and meditated deeply on Kāmadhēnu. In a trice, the forest became a heavenly abode. The trees were transformed into dēvas. There was a sumptuous feast ready for the tired travellers and soft mattresses inside palaces for them to rest upon. Sage Bharadvāja materialized all these through the wish-fulfilling cow, Kāmadhēnu.

"After worshipping Vasiṣṭha, the sage invited the rest of the entourage into His āśram.

"They got up early the next morning, had their morning bath, and prostrated at Sage Bharadvāja's feet. With His blessings, they set off to Citrakūṭa. Bharata instructed the army to remain behind while he, Śatrughna and Guha went in search of Śrī Rāma's āśram. They came across some ascetics who guided them there: 'On the northern bank of the Gangā, by the foothills of the Citrakūṭa Mountains, you will find Śrī Rāma, the supreme self, dwelling there with Sītā and Lakṣmaṇa.'

"The search party soon caught sight of Śrī Rāma's āśram. It was a marvellous place, surrounded by all kinds of trees laden with fruits and by shrubs overhung with fragrant flowers. Birds and beasts lived there in harmony with each other. Bharata flung himself down upon the ground trodden by the feet of Rāma, Sītā and Lakṣmaṇa. As he rushed into the āśram and fell at his elder brother's feet, tears were streaming down his face. With great joy, Śrī Rāma hugged His two brothers. He greeted His three mothers. Sītā prostrated at their feet, and the three mothers hugged Her. They were grieved to see Princess Sītā living in such a rustic place. Śrī Rāma then greeted Sage Vasiṣṭha. 'I hope my father is in good health. Did he send any message for me?'

"The sage answered, 'I'm sorry, Rāma, but your father left this world lamenting for You, Sītā and Lakṣmaṇa.'

"Śrī Rāma sat heavily on the ground, shocked by the news of His father's passing. 'Oh father! Have you abandoned us?' Sītā and Lakṣmaṇa also fell to the ground, unable to bear the shock and sadness that overwhelmed them. Vasiṣṭha consoled them all. Finally, regaining their composure, they went down to the Mandākinī River, where they performed the ceremonial rites for the peace of their father's soul."

“ ***Our life should not be spent in vain. We must live in deference to dharma, to our responsibilities. If we do so, we will not come under the sway of our selfish desires.***

20. Dialogue between Rāma and Bharata

Uṇṇi was waiting in the pūjā room. When Grandma came in, she asked, "Uṇṇi, haven't your exams started? Don't you have a lot to study?"

"No, I have only a bit more to study. I can do that after listening to the story or early tomorrow morning."

Māḷu said, "He will study later, mother. Let us not break the continuity in the narration of the *Rāmāyaṇa*."

Grandma sat with eyes closed and meditated upon Rāma for a minute. She continued, "After the funeral rites were completed, Śrī Rāma and the others returned to the āśram. With great devotion, Bharata beseeched his elder brother, 'Please listen to my request. You are the eldest son of King Daśaratha. You are the rightful heir to the throne. It is not right for you to continue living in the forest. I have brought with me all the materials necessary for the coronation. Please allow me to crown you King of Ayōdhyā. Save the land of Ayōdhyā!'

"Śrī Rāma gently lifted up Bharata, who was lying prostrate before Him, and said, 'I understand all that you say but I am bound by my father's pledge. I shall not disobey him. He pledged the kingdom to you. Therefore,

you must rule the land as its rightful king. I am going to travel to Daṇḍakāraṇya.'

"Bharata repeatedly begged Śrī Rāma to reconsider His decision, but Śrī Rāma stood firm. Deeply hurt, Bharata said, 'In that case, I shall continue living in the forest, serving You, just like Lakṣmaṇa.' When Śrī Rāma denied him this request also, he said, 'In that case, I shall fast to death and abandon my body in this very forest.'

"Bharata spread *darbha* grass (Halfa grass) on the ground and stood under the hot sun, resolving to fast unto death. When Guru Vasiṣṭha understood that Bharata was determined to fulfil his resolve, the sage went to him and said, 'O prince, look at me as I impart a great secret to you! Do not behave like a fool! Reconsider your decision. Your elder brother is none other than the Supreme, Lord Viṣṇu Himself. Sītā Dēvī is the incarnation of Goddess Lakṣmī. You will understand in due course that they are the Creators, the parents of this whole universe. They have been born to destroy Rāvaṇa and the other rākṣasas. The events that led to the 14-year exile in the forest are God's will. Mantharā and Kaikēyī are only instruments in the hands of the Divine. Therefore, abandon the idea of trying to coerce Śrī Rāma back to Ayōdhyā. Seek His blessings and return. After their exile in the forest, Śrī Rāma, Sītā and Lakṣmaṇa will return to Ayōdhyā.'

"Upon hearing the words of Vasiṣṭha, Bharata's heart was filled with wonder. He went near Śrī Rāma and said with great feeling, 'Elder brother, please give me the sandals You wear. They shall represent You and protect the kingdom on Your behalf.'

"Śrī Rāma removed His sandals and gave them to Bharata, who reverentially received them with bowed head. He placed the jewel-encrusted sandals on his head and circumambulated his brother thrice. Then, in a voice heavy with emotion, he said, 'I shall wait 14 years. If you do not return to Ayōdhyā the day after the 14 years are over, I shall enter fire and end my life!'

"Śrī Rāma's eyes filled with tears of love as He reassured His brother, 'Trust me. I shall return to Ayōdhyā the day after my 14-year exile ends.' He then bade farewell to Bharata, who, together with Śatrughna, their three mothers, Guru Vasiṣṭha and his wife, and the great army of Ayōdhyā started their journey back. Guha ferried them back across the mighty Gangā. Bharata and Śatrughna, adopting the attire and the austere life of sages, lived in a place called Nandigrāma. Bharata placed Śrī Rāma's royal sandals on the throne of Ayōdhyā, worshipped the sandals, and ruled the land on His behalf.

"Śrī Rāma, Sītā and Lakṣmaṇa then left Citrakūṭa. They started on their journey to Daṇḍakāraṇya. On the way, they paid obeisance to Anasūya, wife of Sage Atri. Anasūya embraced Sītā and presented Her with resplendent clothes, a pair of exquisite earrings, and fragrant sandalwood paste. The three of them spent the night there, accepting the hospitality of Sage Atri and Anasūya."

> ***Bharata placed and worshipped Śrī Rāma's sandals on the throne, and ruled as regent. The sandals were emblems of the Lord. May rulers always bear in mind the truth that governing a country is equal to worshipping God.***

21. Entering the Dark and Dense Forest

Māḷu and Uṇṇi waited for Grandma to open her eyes. She was meditating on the form of her beautiful Lord, Śrī Rāma. She slowly opened her eyes and looked at the pictures of the gods on the walls of the pūjā room. They seemed to be smiling at the three of them.

Grandma continued, "After a good night's sleep, the three of them woke up before dawn and expressed their desire to enter the dense Daṇḍakāraṇya. Sage Atri blessed them and asked a few young hermits from his āśram to guide them to the forest. They had to ford a river to enter the Daṇḍakāraṇya. The hermits rowed them across the river. After lovingly sending them back, Śrī Rāma, Sītā and Lakṣmaṇa entered the perilous forest, inhabited by cruel beasts, serpents and rākṣasas. Śrī Rāma advised Lakṣmaṇa to string his bow and keep the arrow poised to fly at the slightest hint of danger. Sītā walked in the middle, Rāma protecting Her in front and Lakṣmaṇa keeping watch in the rear. Feeling tired and thirsty, they stopped near a lake, drank their fill of water and then sat back and relaxed under the cool shade of a tree.

"Suddenly, a huge thing bounded up to them with a deafening snarl!"

"What was it, Grandma?" Uṇṇi asked anxiously.

"In one hand, the horrible creature held trees he had uprooted, and in the other hand, he held a blood-smeared spear, laden with impaled animals. The beast snarled, 'Who are you? Who is this lovely princess with you?'

"Śrī Rāma answered, 'I am Rāma and this is my wife Sītā. Lakṣmaṇa is my younger brother. I have come to this forest to kill horrible rākṣasas like you.'

"With great scorn, the rākṣasa uprooted a huge tree and aimed it at Rāma. He said, "I am the invincible Virādha. If you value Your life, flee from this place but let this lovely princess stay here.' Saying so, he darted towards Sītā. Śrī Rāma's arrows lopped off his hands and legs, and finally caused his death. A luminous form rose from the body of Virādha. It circumambulated Śrī Rāma with great devotion and sang His praises. The luminous form said, "I am Vidyādhara, turned into a monstrous rākṣasa by the curse of Sage Durvāsā. By Your mercy, I have been liberated from his curse.'

"Śrī Rāma, Sītā and Lakṣmaṇa continued their journey and reached the hermitage of Sage Śarabhanga. An overjoyed Śarabhanga bowed before Śrī Rāma with great devotion and sang many hymns in His praise. Then, with the three of them watching him, Śarabhanga immolated himself by his yogic powers and ascended to heaven.

"They continued their journey until they reached an area in which many sages lived. The sages could not contain their happiness at seeing Śrī Rāma, who noticed skulls and remnants of bones heaped here and there. He realized that these were the bones of sages killed and eaten by the rākṣasas. Śrī Rāma assured the sages that He would kill the rākṣasas threatening their lives. He told them to meditate and perform their spiritual practices without fear. Śrī Rāma, Lakṣmaṇa and Sītā lived in the forest, protecting these sages, for the next 13 years.

"Once, Śrī Rāma visited a beautiful āśram called Sutīṣṇāśram, wherein lived Sutīṣṇa, a disciple of Sage Agastya. Sutīṣṇa's happiness knew no bounds as he greeted the Lord and escorted Him inside. He worshipped Śrī Rāma and prostrated before him. He said, 'In accordance with my Guru's instructions, I have been living here and constantly chanting the Rāma mantra. I take refuge in You.'

"Śrī Rāma blessed him and told him about His desire to meet Sage Agastya. The following day, all four of them started their journey to Agastya's āśram."

> ***We can cross the ocean of illusion by holding on to the ship of the Lord's feet. Identification with the body binds us to the unending cycle of birth and rebirth. In order to cut the rope that binds us to the world, we must enshrine the Lord in our hearts.***

22. Visiting Sage Agastya and Meeting Jaṭāyu

Grandma called out to Uṇṇi, "Aren't you coming to listen to the *Rāmāyaṇa*? Your mother is already inside the pūjā room. The lamp is lit."

Uṇṇi called out, "Grandma, I was playing in the garden. Let me wash my hands, legs and face first. I'll be there in a minute!"

Grandma smiled, happy at the thought that Uṇṇi had made cleanliness a habit in his life. She and Māḷu then started chanting Rāma's name until Uṇṇi arrived.

"Grandma, I have come."

Uṇṇi snuggled close to his grandmother. She kissed him on his wet forehead. "Do you remember where we stopped, Uṇṇi?" She asked her grandson.

"Yes, Grandma. Sutīṣṇa is taking Rāma, Sītā and Lakṣmaṇa to the hermitage of Sage Agastya."

"Who was Agastya?" asked Grandma.

"Sutīṣṇa's Guru!" replied Uṇṇi promptly.

"You're right! The four of them walked until they reached a divine forest. Many āśrams were situated there. It was among the most beautiful places they had seen. Flowers of all seasons bloomed there. Trees were laden with fruit. A wide variety of animals lived together harmoniously. The melodious warbling of different birds enlivened this enchanting scene.

"They continued walking, marvelling at the beauty of the forest. Finally, they reached Sage Agastya's āśram. The three of them waited outside as Sutīṣṇa hastened to inform his Guru of Śrī Rāma's arrival. Sage Agastya was thrilled by the news that Śrī Rāma, whom he worshipped constantly in the temple of his heart, had come to see him. Together with his disciples, the sage hastened towards the Lord. He had spent years waiting for Śrī Rāma, and in all those years, his heart had been constantly murmuring Śrī Rāma's name. When he saw Rāma, he said, 'My life has been fulfilled!'

"Rāma, Sītā and Lakṣmaṇa were surprised at Agastya's devotion as he hastened to meet and welcome them. They prostrated in front of the great sage. Agastya's eyes were brimming with tears. He worshipped Śrī Rāma and offered Him the most delicious fruits and nuts. He said, 'O Śrī Rāma, from the day You were born, I have been waiting patiently to see You. I have been chanting Your name and mentally worshipping Your divine feet since then.'

"He sang many songs glorifying Śrī Rāma. These devotional hymns were based on the principle of God as the ultimate reality, the infinite truth. His hymns dwelt on the creation of the universe, knowledge of the Self, and the power of devotion. After singing many hymns, the sage prayed earnestly to Rāma, 'O Lord, may my mind remain constantly absorbed in You, and may my love and devotion increase day by day. May You remain ever fresh in my heart as I walk, sit and perform each and every action.' After praying thus, he brought a divine bow, arrows and a quiver that Indra, the chief of the gods, had entrusted him long ago, and offered them to Śrī Rāma. He prayed, 'May Your hands be able to destroy the evil rākṣasas easily!' He then said, 'A short distance away is a hallowed spot called Pañcavaṭī. Go there and build an āśram on the banks of Gautamī River.'

"Śrī Rāma listened attentively to the sagely advice and to the hymns of praise he had sung. He put down the bow and arrows presented to him, and prostrated before Sage Agastya.

"After bidding the sage farewell, Rāma, Sītā and Lakṣmaṇa set out for Pañcavaṭī. As they were walking, they saw lying before them the noble eagle Jaṭāyu, huge as a mountain. Śrī Rāma did not recognize the eagle. Calling Lakṣmaṇa, he said, 'I think a huge rākṣasa is lying in wait for the sages passing this way so that he can devour them. Pass me my bow and arrows. I shall finish him off at once!'

"Hearing this, Jaṭāyu became afraid. He said, 'O Rāmacandra, please do not kill me. I am Your devotee, Jaṭāyu. In my younger days, I was your father's friend.'

"Hearing this, Rāmacandra hugged the huge bird and blessed him. He said, 'O king of birds! Come and live near our āśram. Have no more fear.' Rāma felt sad that He had mistaken Jaṭāyu for a rākṣasa. Walking along, they reached Pañcavaṭī."

“ ***Once upon a time, there were many divine forests on earth, like the one in which Sage Agastya's āśram was situated. Now, they have all become the stuff of legends. There are no more great forests filled with lovely creepers, magnificent trees and wild animals and birds of all kinds. Owing to our ignorance and selfishness, we have cut down the great forests. We know that forests are essential for the sustenance of humanity. It is our duty to protect the forests and the environment. Let us plant more trees. Let us aspire to have such great forests grace the face of earth once again. Let that be our goal.***

23. Reaching the Pañcavaṭī, Arrival of Śūrpaṇakhā

Grandmother, Māḷu and Uṇṇi came together in the evening, when the lamps were lit in the pūjā room. Grandma continued with the story of Prince Rāma.

"As soon as Śrī Rāma, Sītā and Lakṣmaṇa reached Pañcavaṭī, Lakṣmaṇa built a home of bamboo and leaves for Rāma and Sītā, by the banks of Gautamī River. For Śrī Rāma, Lakṣmaṇa made a floral mattress. They started living in happiness and peace in the āśram situated amidst banana, mango, jackfruit and many other fruit-bearing trees. Theirs was a life of discipline.

"One day, Lakṣmaṇa requested Śrī Rāma to reveal to him the principle of ultimate reality and the goal of life. The answers that Śrī Rāma gave are found in the *'Lakṣmaṇōpadēśa'* section in the *Rāmāyaṇa*. Śrī Rāma talks about devotion to God and knowledge of the Self residing within each one of us."

Looking at Uṇṇi, Grandma said, "Uṇṇi, this is something you must read and understand for yourself. You are too young to understand the wisdom and depth of Śrī Rāma's words. The advice given to Lakṣmaṇa gives one knowledge of the supreme self, which we call God. Repeated reading allows us to understand better the wisdom of the Lord's words. He gives paramount importance to having devotion to God.

"After Śrī Rāma advised Lakṣmaṇa on the true nature of the Self, they rested in the shade. It was then that it happened, the incident that was to become instrumental in Rāma's slaying of Rāvaṇa: the arrival of a shape-changing *rākṣasī* (demoness)! As she was wandering along the bank of the Gautamī, she noticed an attractive trail of footprints, attractive because the footprints had the imprint of the lotus on them. They were the footprints of Lord Rāma. She thought, 'If the footprints are so beautiful, then the man to whom it belongs must be exceedingly handsome!' She followed the footprints until she reached Śrī Rāma's hut. There, she saw Śrī Rāma sitting beside Sītā. The desire to marry him arose in her mind. Changing her hideous form into that of a lissome damsel, she approached Rāma and asked Him, 'O worthy prince! Who are you? Whose son are you? Why have you come here to this forest? Why are you wearing the bark of a tree? Why is your hair matted? Let me introduce myself. I am the sister of Rāvaṇa, the mighty king of the rākṣasas. My name is Śūrpaṇakhā. I can change my form at will. I have three other strong brothers: Khara, Dūṣaṇa and Triśiras. Now tell me about yourself.'

"Śrī Rāma answered her, "O beautiful lady, I am Śrī Rāma, the son of King Daśaratha of Ayōdhyā. You see my younger brother Lakṣmaṇa standing over there. Beside me is my wife, Sītā.'

"Hearing this, Śūrpaṇakhā said, 'O valiant prince, I find it impossible to leave your company! Please accept me as your wife.'

"Glancing mischievously at Sītā, Śrī Rāma said, 'I am a nomad wandering from one forest to another. I am also married. I cannot abandon my wife. Having more than one wife will create misunderstandings. You won't be able to tolerate the misunderstandings. My younger brother, standing over there, is handsome, and you are rich and beautiful. You will be a good match for each other. Go and share with him your desire.'

"As soon as Śrī Rāma finished speaking, Śūrpaṇakhā approached Lakṣmaṇa and asked him to marry her. Lakṣmaṇa smiled and said, 'I am Śrī Rāmacandra's servant. If you marry me, you will become a mere servant, whereas you are fit to be a queen! Convince my elder brother of your sterling qualities. I am sure He will accept you!'

"Śūrpaṇakhā was bent on fulfilling her desire at any cost. Returning to Śrī Rāma, she said, 'I will make a perfect wife. We can travel over all the forests and cities, and live a carefree life.'

"Śrī Rāma said, 'A man needs a woman to take care of his needs, and I already have a princess who takes care of me wonderfully well. We were searching for a princess for my younger brother, and you came as an answer to our prayers. Go back to him. I am sure he will accept you!'

"When Śūrpaṇakhā returned to Lakṣmaṇa, he scolded her, "Hey rākṣasī! I have no love for you. Go back to Śrī Rāmacandra!'

"When Śūrpaṇakhā returned to Śrī Rāma, all her anger and frustration were directed towards Sītā, whom she considered the cause of her thwarted desire. Assuming her natural form — black and as big as a mountain — she rushed with her mouth wide open, revealing jagged canines, towards Sītā, intending to devour her. Śrī Rāma blocked the murderous rākṣasī, as Lakṣmaṇa, quick as lightning, reached His side and lopped off her nose and ears. Howling in pain and rage, the rākṣasī ran away."

Uṇṇi asked, "Grandma, Rāma and Lakṣmaṇa were trying to deflect her purpose, weren't they?"

Grandmother and Māḷu said yes.

> ***Even if we have eyes to see, we will not be able to see anything without light. Devotion is like a lighted lamp. Without the lamp of devotion, one will not be able to see the path to Self-knowledge. One cannot achieve spiritual liberation without devotion.***

24. Killing of Khara, Lament of Śūrpaṇakhā

Grandmother continued the story, "Uṇṇi, when Śūrpaṇakhā ran away into the woods, screaming, Śrī Rāma told Lakṣmaṇa, 'This might be an impelling reason for the King of Lanka, Rāvaṇa, to start a fight with us.'"

Uṇṇi asked, "Where did the rākṣasī run away to?"

"She ran screaming to her brother, Khara. When he saw his sister disfigured and crying in pain and anger, he asked her, 'Who did this to you?'

"Śūrpaṇakhā said, 'Two sons of King Daśaratha, most handsome and skilled in weaponry, live in this forest. There is a woman named Sītā with them. It was in obedience to his elder brother's command that Lakṣmaṇa, the younger brother, disfigured me. Kill them and bring me their flesh, dripping with fresh blood, for me to eat and drink. Only then will I feel avenged!"

"Hearing this, Khara at once sent 14 strong rākṣasas to kill the two brothers. Śūrpaṇakhā went ahead to show them the way and to point out the princes.

"Uṇṇi, do you know what the weapons were that they carried with them? Spears, thorny branches, iron pestles, sword, bows and arrows, and slingshots, among others. Drawing close to Śrī Rāma, they loosed all their weapons on Him. He calmly fended off their attacks, and killed all of them. Alarmed by this disastrous turn of events, Śūrpaṇakhā ran back to Khara and informed him of what had happened. A furious Khara assembled an army of a thousand rākṣasas, and, with his brothers Dūṣaṇa and

Triśiras, set out to fight against the two brothers. Rāma, knowing that a fierce and deadly battle was going to erupt, comforted Lakṣmaṇa: 'Do not be afraid. Escort Sītā into a cave and stand guard. I shall face and defeat these monsters alone.'

"After escorting Sītā into a cave, Lakṣmaṇa stood outside, alert for any danger. The attacking horde of rākṣasas rolled in like sea waves and rained weapons on Lord Rāma. He first killed Dūṣaṇa, and then severed Triśiras's three heads with a single arrow. When he saw that both his brothers had fallen, Khara charged at the Lord. They fought with each other for a long time. Khara was extraordinarily powerful, and inflicted wounds all over Rāma's body by a constant barrage of weapons. Rāma then used the bow and arrow that Sage Agastya had given him, and cut asunder all the weapons Khara used against Him. Finally, Śrī Rāma shot a divine arrow and beheaded Khara, causing the severed head to land in Rāvaṇa's court in Lanka!

"When she saw her strong brothers being killed, Śūrpaṇakhā fainted. All the rākṣasas whom Śrī Rāma killed attained *mōkṣa* (spiritual liberation). After making sure that all their enemies were dead, Lakṣmaṇa and Sītā went to Śrī Rāma. Lakṣmaṇa bowed down before Rāma. When Sītā saw that Rāma's body was riddled with wounds, Her eyes welled up with tears of sorrow. Softly and gently, Sītā caressed the lacerations on Rāma's body.

As She did so, they disappeared. Rāma's body became whole once again.

"The sages rejoiced when they heard that Rāma had vanquished the rākṣasas. They created a divine body armour that they presented Rāma, along with a ring and a crest jewel, the *cūḍāmaṇi*. Śrī Rāma gave the body armour to Lakṣmaṇa, the cūḍāmaṇi to Sītā, and wore the ring Himself.

"When she regained consciousness, Śūrpaṇakhā fled to Lanka, where she poured out her tale of woe to her eldest brother, Rāvaṇa, King of Lanka. She recounted the defeat and death of Dūṣaṇa, Triśiras and Khara at the hands of Śrī Rāma. The wily and vindictive rākṣasī then concocted a story to win Rāvaṇa over: 'I was enjoying the scenery of Pañcavaṭī while strolling along the banks of the Gautamī. There I saw Princes Rāma and Lakṣmaṇa, sons of King Daśaratha. Śrī Rāma's wife, Sītā, was with them. She is lovely beyond imagination. I cannot imagine a beauty and tenderness that can rival Sītā's in this whole world. I tried to abduct that peerless beauty and present Her to you. But obeying the command of his brother, Lakṣmaṇa chopped off my nose and ears, and thus disfigured me. They also killed our brothers. Abduct Sītā and bring Her to Lanka. Marry Her. You will become king of the world. But remember, you will never be able to win Her in a battle with Rāma. Abduct Her using a clever ruse.'

"The desire for Sītā was planted in Rāvaṇa's mind. He wanted to marry Her. He then worked out a clever plan."

> ***Nothing is impossible for incarnations of God. Nevertheless, all of them face the same difficulties of life that an ordinary human being encounters. The path they walk in order to fulfil their divine mission is never easy but outright thorny. The lives of divine incarnations teach us how to face and overcome the difficulties and obstacles we face in life.***

25. Slaying of Mārīca and Abduction of Sītā

Uṇṇi was anxious and upset. He wanted to hear more. "What happened?" he asked his grandmother. "What did Rāvaṇa do?"

"Rāvaṇa reflected, 'Śrī Rāma is not a mere mortal, for He vanquished and killed Khara, Dūṣaṇa and Triśiras. Maybe, He is Lord Viṣṇu Himself, born on earth to kill me.' He decided he would confront Lord Rāma. 'If I win the war, the loveliest princess in all the three worlds will be mine, and I will become unrivalled in glory. Suppose I lose the war. What then? If I die at the hands of Lord Viṣṇu, I shall definitely attain mōkṣa and reach His abode, Vaikuṇṭha. Because I will benefit either way, let me try abducting Sītā.'

"Rāvaṇa went straight to Mārīca, who welcomed him warmly and inquired about the reason for the royal visit. Rāvaṇa replied, 'We have been greatly humiliated. The sons of Daśaratha, princes Rāma and Lakṣmaṇa, along with Sītā are staying in the pathless, trackless, boundless Daṇḍaka forest. Without any provocation, Lakṣmaṇa disfigured my sister Śūrpaṇakhā. You must take on the form of a golden-coloured deer and cast a magic spell on Sītā. She will request Her husband to "follow the deer." You must find a way to separate and distance Rāma and Lakṣmaṇa from Sītā. If this ruse succeeds, I shall be able to abduct Sītā and bring Her over here. You must help me in this.'

"Hearing the words of Rāvaṇa, Mārīca felt a sense of dread. He remembered the fate that had befallen the rākṣasas who tried to obstruct the yajña of Sage Viśvāmitra. Mārīca was still alive only because Śrī Rāma had forgiven him. Since then, Mārīca had become a loving devotee of Śrī Rāma. Mārīca advised Rāvaṇa, 'Lord Rāma is the incarnation of Viṣṇu, born to kill you. Hence, instead of trying to fight him or oppose him, live as a devotee of Rāma.' Rāvaṇa resented Mārīca's wise advice and threatened to kill him. Mārīca thought, 'Better to die at the hands of Lord Rāma while impersonating a deer than at the hands of this monster!' He agreed to obey Rāvaṇa's command.

"With his magical powers, Mārīca took on the form of an enchanting golden deer. None could resist its captivating charm. The golden deer started gambolling near the āśram. Sītā was captivated by the deer's frolicking, and requested Śrī Rāma to capture it so that She could play with and take care of the deer.

"Śrī Rāma wanted to fulfil His lovely wife's desire. Before setting out in search of the golden deer, He instructed Lakṣmaṇa to guard Sītā. Lakṣmaṇa tried to dissuade his brother from going after the golden deer, saying that it was a rākṣasa who had assumed this enchanting form. He sensed grave danger for the three of them. But as Sītā was uncharacteristically adamant, Śrī Rāma set out in search of the golden deer that was playing hide and seek at a far distance. The magic deer eluded Śrī Rāma and led him further and further inside the deep forest. Finally, when Śrī Rāma realized that the deer could not be caught bare-handed, He shot an arrow at the deer.

"At once, the deer assumed its real form. Imitating the voice of Śrī Rāma, he cried out in distress, 'O Lakṣmaṇa, my brother, save me!' Mārīca then fell dead. A terrified Sītā, hearing the call, begged Lakṣmaṇa to run to his brother's aid. Lakṣmaṇa replied, "It is not Rāma's voice, but the clever ruse of a rākṣasa. My brother has instructed me to not to leave Your side. So I am staying here to protect You.'

"However, fear for Her husband's safety overpowered Sītā's better judgement. She said that She would kill Herself if Lakṣmaṇa did not go to the aid of his brother, and even accused him of wishing his brother dead! Hurt by the accusations that Sītā was hurling at him, Lakṣmaṇa, with many misgivings, left Her, and went in search of Rāma.

"Rāvaṇa, who was watching everything from up in the skies, assumed the form of a *sanyāsī* (ordained monk) and approached the āśram. Sītā greeted him respectfully. The sanyāsī asked Her, "Who are you? Who is your husband?'

"She answered, 'I am Sītā, daughter of King Janaka. My husband is Prince Rāma, son of King Daśaratha of Ayōdhyā. His younger brother Lakṣmaṇa is also with us.'

"Rāvaṇa said, 'I am Rāvaṇa, King of Lanka. Why do You, who are so lovely and fair, suffer the hardships of life in this dense forest? Abandon Your husband, who is garbed like an ascetic, and take me, the King of Lanka, as your husband. You shall become Empress of Lanka!'

"Rāvaṇa's words filled Sītā with fear and loathing. She said, 'My husband and his brother will arrive now, and they will kill you!'

"Sītā's rejection and Her warning made Rāvaṇa tremble with anger. He assumed his real form. Seeing his 10 heads and 20 hands, Sītā began trembling in fear. The guardian angels of the forest were petrified at the sight of his fearsome form. Rāvaṇa then grabbed Sītā and pulled Her into his *puṣpaka-vimāna* (flying chariot), which flew up into the skies and made its way to Lanka."

> ***Sītā did not heed Lakṣmaṇa's counsel. Her sharp words drove him to Śrī Rāma. Rāvaṇa did not heed Mārīca's warning and abducted Sītā. All this was part of the Lord's plan to destroy Rāvaṇa.***

26. Searching for Sītā, Meeting Jaṭāyu

Grandma continued with the story. "Rāvaṇa's puṣpaka-vimāna flew into the skies with Sītā Dēvī."

Uṇṇi said in a low and sad voice, "How horrible! If only Sītā had listened to Lakṣmaṇa, She would have been safe, and nothing so horrible would have happened!"

Grandma pulled Uṇṇi close to her, and smiled at her innocent grandson. "All that happens is God's will, Uṇṇi. Śrī Rāma needed a reason to destroy Rāvaṇa. There has to be a reason for every action. Śrī Rāma could not just have walked into Lanka and told Rāvaṇa, 'Hey, I have come to kill you. Let's fight!'"

"True," Uṇṇi agreed and started laughing. Grandmother and Māḷu joined in the laughter. "What happened afterwards?" Uṇṇi asked.

"As the puṣpaka-vimāna was flying, Sītā cried out, "O Rāma, O Lakṣmaṇa, save me! Rāvaṇa is taking me away with him! Save me, O Rāma!' The king of birds, Jaṭāyu, the huge eagle, was resting in the forest. Hearing Sītā's cries, he looked up and saw Rāvaṇa carrying Lord Rāma's consort away. At once, he flew into the air, his huge wings bearing him swiftly up to Rāvaṇa. Jaṭāyu looked like a winged mountain. He hit the puṣpaka-vimāna with his powerful wings, causing it to stop mid-air. With his mighty talons, Jaṭāyu broke into pieces the arrows that Rāvaṇa shot at him. With his sharp beak, the powerful eagle broke the front of the puṣpaka-vimāna. Furious at being challenged in his attempt to carry Sītā away,

Rāvaṇa fought back brutally. The two titans thus clashed in mid-air, Rāvaṇa, the rākṣasa king, and Jaṭāyu, the king of birds. Finally, Rāvaṇa used the *candrahāsa*, the gleaming scimitar, to slice away both wings of Jaṭāyu. The old bird fell helpless to the ground as the puṣpaka-vimāna tore away to its destination. Seeing this, a tearful Sītā blessed Jaṭāyu, 'May you remain alive until my husband passes this way and you are able to recount to Him what happened.'

"Moaning in pain, Jaṭāyu waited for Śrī Rāma's arrival. Sītā sat still in the puṣpaka-vimāna, meditating upon Her dear Lord. Tears were streaming down Her face incessantly.

"After they had flown a long distance, Sītā spied five monkeys on a mountain peak. She quickly took off Her ornaments, tore off half Her shawl, and made a bundle of the ornaments with it. Throwing them down with great force, She prayed, 'May my husband be able to find these.'

"Rāvaṇa did not notice what Sītā had done. They crossed the seas without any delay and the chariot flew straight to the Aśōka Grove situated in the middle of Rāvaṇa's palace. Sītā alighted from the chariot and took refuge in the shade of a *Śimśapa* tree. Many rākṣasīs guarded Her throughout the day and night. Sītā sat there, absorbed in meditating on Her Lord, foregoing food and sleep, braving hot days and cold nights, wind and rain. She was immensely sad.

"Now, let us turn back to Rāma and Lakṣmaṇa. After killing Mārīca, Rāma was hurrying back to Sītā. When He saw Lakṣmaṇa approaching Him from afar, Rāma said, 'Lakṣmaṇa, the golden deer was Mārīca, the conjurer. I killed him. Why have you come to me? Why did you leave Sītā alone?'

"Lakṣmaṇa cried as he told Rāma about the events leading to his coming in search of his elder brother. 'Elder brother,' said Lakṣmaṇa, 'I tried to convince Sītā that the cries for help came from a rākṣasa who knew how to imitate Your voice, but Sītā Dēvī wasn't ready to listen to me. She accused me of evil designs. That's why I left Her alone and came in search of You. Forgive me!'

"Rāma broke into a run. Lakṣmaṇa ran along. When they reached the āśram, Sītā was nowhere to be seen. Rāma called out, his voice breaking in anxiety, 'Sītā, O Sītā, where are You?' He searched frantically all around the āśram. Not knowing where to go, the brothers went searching for Sītā all over the forest. They saw the broken parts of a chariot and weapons. In a deeply pained voice, Rāma asked Lakṣmaṇa, 'Has any rākṣasa abducted my Sītā, killed Her and eaten Her?'

"It was then that they saw a terrible form lying motionless nearby. Thinking that he was the rākṣasa who had eaten Sītā, Rāma rushed towards him, ready to kill him. It was Jaṭāyu, lying waiting patiently for the arrival of his Lord, Śrī Rāma. He addressed Śrī Rāma, 'O Rāma, do not kill me! I am Jaṭāyu, the friend of your father, Daśaratha. I saw Rāvaṇa travelling through the air in his aerial chariot, carrying Sītā Dēvī away. I heard Her cry out for you and Lakṣmaṇa. I flew into the air to challenge Rāvaṇa. After a long fight, he sliced off my wings with the candrahāsa. Sītā Dēvī blessed me, giving me life until You met me and I recounted the story to you.'

"Even while suffering unimaginable pain, Jaṭāyu was happily gazing deeply at the beautiful face of his Lord. He then sang hymns in praise of Śrī Rāma. The Lord gently hoisted the huge bird onto His lap, and tenderly caressed the noble bird. In deep bliss, Jaṭāyu abandoned his body and attained union with his Lord. Śrī Rāma built a pyre for the brave bird and cremated him. He also performed his last rites, as befitting a noble human."

> ***Those who are established in the bliss of the Self will not be affected by joy and sorrow. Yet, as He had incarnated as a human, Śrī Rāma felt all the emotions of a noble person. He became distraught at the loss of His dear Sītā, and was inconsolable.***

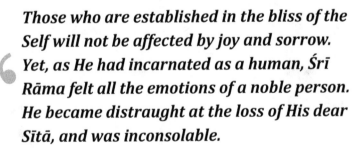

27. Kabandha's Story, Visiting Śabarī's Āśram

Grandmother continued with the story of Śrī Rāma. Uṇṇi and his mother listened to her with bated breath.

"Thus, Jaṭāyu attained mōkṣa. Accompanied by Lakṣmaṇa, Śrī Rāma continued to roam the forests, pining for Sītā. Suddenly, they saw in front of them a grotesque creature on the ground. The creature's face was in its chest but one could not see its eyes. It was neither a bird nor a beast. It had neither head nor legs. However, it had very long arms, which were twitching.

Uṇṇi said, "What a scary creature, Grandma!"

"Yes, Uṇṇi. Even Śrī Rāma was astounded. It was a rākṣasa by name of Kabandha. Rāma said, 'Lakṣmaṇa, we are trapped inside the arms of this creature. I see no way of escape. We are going to be gobbled up!'

"Lakṣmaṇa thought and bravely replied, 'Elder brother, I shall slice off one of its arms. You do the same to the other arm.'

"Without wasting any more time, Śrī Rāma sliced off the creature's right arm and Lakṣmaṇa severed its left. The creature asked them, 'Who are you? None before you have had the strength to cut away my arms. Tell me why you have entered this forest.'

"Śrī Rāma said, 'I am the eldest son of King Daśaratha of Ayōdhyā. This is my younger brother, Lakṣmaṇa. Cruel rākṣasas abducted my wife Sītā while we were away. We are travelling from forest to forest, searching for Her. Tell us who you are.'

"When it spoke, the creature's voice did not have any anger or pain. In fact, there was a certain joy in its tone. 'I was a handsome *gandharva* (celestial being). Once I teased Sage Aṣṭavakra about his deformed body.'"

"Grandma, why did he make fun of a sage?" asked Uṇṇi.

"Aṣṭavakra's body was twisted in eight places. Kabandha had laughed in derision, seeing its peculiar shape. He was also conceited about his good looks. The angry sage cursed him, 'May you became a rākṣasa! In the *Trētā Yuga,*[11] Śrī Rāma will come and chop off your hands. Only then will you become free of your curse.'

"Thus the handsome Gandharva became a rākṣasa. Once, he fought with Indra, king of heaven, who cut his neck off, put his face on his chest, and stuffed his head and legs inside his body. Only his long hands were able to move freely. From that day onwards, Kabandha survived by grabbing and eating any creature that came its way.

"After recounting his story, the creature requested Śrī Rāma, 'Please cremate this body of mine. Afterwards, I shall offer suggestions on where to search for Sītā.'

"Kabandha died. Śrī Rāma cremated his body. A divine form arose from the flames. Kabandha regained his earlier form of a handsome gandharva. Kabandha prostrated before Rāma and sang His praises. The hymn

11 Second of four ages that characterize one cycle of the universe (from origin to dissolution).

he sang was so beautiful that Śrī Rāma was pleased with the depth of the gandharva's devotion. Blessing Kabandha, He said, 'Those who pray to me by singing your hymn will attain liberation.'

"Kabandha humbly told the Lord, 'O noble One! Nearby is the Gautamāśram. A sage by name Śabarī lives there, absorbed in meditating on Your form. If you meet her, she will tell you in which direction You must go in search of Sītā.'

"With those words, the gandharva disappeared. Śrī Rāma and Lakṣmaṇa reached the āśram of Śabarī by the banks of River Pampā. On seeing the Lord, the aged Śabarī greeted them and bade them sit. She washed the feet of her Lord and sprinkled the holy water on her head. She performed pūjā to her Lord, fed Him with fruits and water, and sang many songs glorifying Him. She said, 'I am an old and foolish woman, born in a low caste. O my glorious Lord, what right do I have to sing Your praises?'

"Śrī Rāma answered, 'To attain the Lord, what is essential is unalloyed devotion. Whether you are a man or a woman is of no consequence.' He then said, 'O sage! Please help me. I need to know where to go in search of my wife Sītā.'

"Śabarī had divine sight and thus knew everything. She said, 'I know that there is nothing in this world that you are unaware of, and yet because You have incarnated as a human being and are asking me for news, I shall tell

You. Sītā Dēvī is sitting in a grove of Aśōka trees in the land of Lanka across the seas. She is meditating sadly on Your divine form. Rāvaṇa abducted Her. Go to the Ṛṣyamukha mountain range. Sugrīva, the monkey, is living in exile there with four of his monkey ministers. He is afraid of his bigger brother Vālī. Forge an alliance with Sugrīva. Then all that You have come for will be easily achieved.'

"Śabarī closed her eyes and started chanting the Śrī Rāma mantra. Using her yogic powers, she merged into the fire she created from within. Thus Śabarī attained mōkṣa."

> ***Śrī Rāma is a treasure trove of compassion. He grants liberation to anyone devoted to Him. There is no need to perform yajñas or to practise intense meditation. Constantly chant the Rāma mantra, and know that the Lord is the pure consciousness pervading the entire universe.***

28. Meeting Hanumān, Friendship with Sugrīva

Grandmother said, "Uṇṇi, we are now entering the Kiṣkindhā section of the *Rāmāyaṇa*. Following Śabarī's advice, Śrī Rāma and Lakṣmaṇa started on the long journey to the Ṛṣyamukha mountain ranges. When they reached the banks of the Pampā, they saw wild animals like the lion and leopard coming to quench their thirst at the river, which abounded with pink and red lotuses. Swans and water hens swam around and the place buzzed with many busy bees. Śrī Rāma and Lakṣmaṇa drank from the clear waters and slowly moved forward. The gentle breeze wafted the fragrance of the flowers adorning the trees. Śrī Rāma felt sad thinking of Sītā, who was not beside Him to enjoy the gentle breeze and the beauty of the forest. He talked to Lakṣmaṇa as they journeyed on their way to the Ṛṣyamukha mountain range.

"Someone was watching them closely as they approached the mountain. Do you know who it was? It was Sugrīva. Uṇṇi, you remember Sugrīva, don't you?"

Uṇṇi said, "Of course. Sugrīva was hiding in the mountain because he was scared of his elder brother Vālī."

Patting him on his back, Māḷu said, "Uṇṇi, you are really listening to the narration with great interest and concentration!"

Affectionately caressing the young boy's cheeks, Grandma continued. "When Sugrīva saw the two strangers approaching the mountain, he ran for life. He collected his four ministers and they swiftly climbed up to the mountain peak. He addressed Hanumān, 'Hey Vāyuputra, son of the Wind! Two young men carrying weapons are coming this way. They look so radiant! Why are they coming this way? Could it be that my brother has sent them? Have they come to finish me off? Go to them. Secretly find out who they are. Show me some sign to indicate whether they are friends or enemies.'

"Assuming the form of a Brāhmin, Hanumān went up to Rāma and Lakṣmaṇa and greeted them with palms joined reverentially. 'O handsome youths! You seem to be gods who have come down to earth as mortals. You are surrounded by an aura of divine radiance. Please tell me why you have come to these mountains.'

"Śrī Rāma said, 'O great soul! We are sons of King Daśaratha of Ayōdhyā. My wife Sītā Dēvī was with us. We had come to the Daṇḍaka Forest to meditate and live the life of ascetics at the behest of our father. Cruel rākṣasas abducted Sītā Dēvī. We are going from forest to forest in search of Her. So far, our search has been in vain. Now, please tell us about yourself.'

"Hanumān assumed his real form and humbly bowed down to the two of them. He said, 'The monkey king named Sugrīva is living on top of this mountain. Four of us, his loyal ministers, are with him. His elder brother, Vālī, abducted Sugrīva's wife and chased us out of the kingdom. A sage once cursed Vālī: if he ever entered the Ṛṣyamukha mountain range, his head would explode.

That is why Vālī does not dare come here. Sugrīva is safe in this hideout. It will benefit both of you to make a pact with Sugrīva to destroy each other's enemies and help one other.'

"Hanumān then hoisted Rāma and Lakṣmaṇa onto his strong shoulders and carried them up to the mountain peak. He told Sugrīva, 'O Sugrīva, son of the Sun God! Fear no more! Rāma and Lakṣmaṇa are gods who have incarnated as human beings in the Sun dynasty. Rāma's wife, Sītā Dēvī, was abducted by a rākṣasa. The princes have been travelling from forest to forest, looking for Her. Bow down before them and offer to make a pact.'

"Sugrīva prostrated before Rāma. Lakṣmaṇa gave him a brief rundown of events. After hearing Lakṣmaṇa out, Sugrīva assured Rāma, 'Trust me, I shall search for and find Sītā Dēvī for You. Consider me Your own. If it is Rāvaṇa who has abducted Her, I shall see to the destruction of his whole race. This is my solemn pledge!'

"He then told Rāma what he had seen recently. 'One day, we saw a beautiful lady being carried away through the skies by a rākṣasa. She was crying out, "Rāma! Rāma!" When she saw us, she bundled some ornaments in a piece of cloth and threw the bundle down. I have kept it safe.'

"Sugrīva then brought the bundle and placed it in front of Rāma. As soon as Rāma saw the ornaments, tears began streaming down his face. As He sobbed like an ordinary mortal, He turned to his brother. 'Lakṣmaṇa, look! Aren't these my Sītā's ornaments?'

"Lakṣmaṇa replied, 'The anklets are Hers. I see them every day when I bow down to Her.'

"Sugrīva and Lakṣmaṇa tried to console the grief-stricken Rāma. Selecting an auspicious time, Hanumān kindled a fire. In the presence of the fire, with the divine flames as witness, Śrī Rāma and Sugrīva made a pact of friendship. They believed that this pact would help them both regain the precious things they had lost in their lives."

> ***Even the strongest person needs the help of others at some point in his or her life. Even an incarnation of God needed the help of another to achieve His ends. If we have to form friendships, let it be with good people.***

29. Cause of Rift between Vālī and Sugrīva

Uṇṇi asked his grandmother, "Grandma, why did Vālī want to kill Sugrīva? Isn't Sugrīva his younger brother? Why should someone want to kill his own brother?"

"Uṇṇi, that was the same question Śrī Rāma asked Sugrīva: 'What is the cause of your enmity?'

"Sugrīva recounted the events leading up to the ill feelings between the two brothers. Once, an arrogant rākṣasa by name Māyāvī challenged Vālī to a fight. Enraged by the challenge, Vālī punched the rākṣasa hard. Realizing that Vālī was stronger than him, Māyāvī ran for life. Vālī wanted to kill the rākṣasa, who was also a great conjurer, and ran after him. Sugrīva ran after Vālī, wanting to help his brother if necessary. Māyāvī ran inside a cave that went underground. Vālī followed him. But before entering the deep cave, Vālī turned to Sugrīva and said, 'Brother, stay here and keep watch. I shall hunt for the rākṣasa and kill him! If milk flows out of this cave, know that the rākṣasa has been killed. If blood flows out of the cave, beware imminent danger. Block the mouth to the cave, and rule the kingdom.'

"Sugrīva faithfully kept watch outside the cave. Even after a month, Vālī did not return. One day, blood started flowing out from the mouth of the cave. Sugrīva was grieved, thinking that his elder brother had been killed by the rākṣasa. He closed the cave mouth with huge boulders so that Māyāvī could not escape. He returned to the kingdom and informed the court and councillors about his elder brother's passing. The kingdom observed a period of mourning. Then Sugrīva was crowned king.

"After a long time, Vālī reappeared. He believed that Sugrīva had closed the mouth of the cave in order to kill him. He was not interested in hearing his brother's explanation. Vālī was so furious that he charged at Sugrīva, intending to kill him. Sugrīva ran for life. Vālī pursued him with a vengeance. Sugrīva ran and ran until he reached the Ṛṣyamukha mountains.

"Vālī could not enter these mountains because of the curse. It was the only place Sugrīva could rest without fear of being tracked down. He then told Rāma, 'My brother has even made my wife his own. I have lost my country, my home and my wife. O Lord! You must save me!'

"Śrī Rāma consoled him, 'Do not grieve. I shall kill your enemy and hand you the kingdom, wealth and your wife.'

"Sugrīva rejoiced on hearing Śrī Rāma's words, but added hesitantly, 'Lord, it's not easy to kill Vālī, the son of Indra. Once, an asura named Dundubhi challenged Vālī to a fight. Dundubhi had assumed the form a fiendish buffalo. Vālī grabbed his sharp horns, wrestled him down, and keeping him down with one leg, yanked his neck out and hurled it away. The bull's neck and face fell here. At that time, Mātanga Maharṣi's āśram was situated here. The blood from the bull's severed neck defiled the āśram and its surroundings. The furious sage cursed Vālī: if Vālī ever came to this mountain, his head would explode. That's why I'm living here without any fear. Look yonder, my Lord. You can see Dundubhi's head strewn there like a black mountain. Only one who is strong enough to pick up that monstrous head and throw it away can kill Vālī.'

"Rāma smiled at Sugrīva's words and his look of hesitation. Stretching out His leg, Rāma used his big toe to flick the huge skeletal head. It flew into the air and fell a hundred miles away. Awed by the Lord's might, Sugrīva bowed before Him joyfully.

"But there was one more challenge to be overcome. Sugrīva pointed out seven great trees forming a circle. 'Vālī uses these seven trees to test his strength. When he shakes those trees, all their leaves fall down. If my Lord can cut through those seven trees with a single arrow, Vālī is certain to be defeated.'

"Without the slightest hesitation, Śrī Rāma shot an arrow that uprooted all seven trees and continued on its course, penetrating the mountain and the earth, before returning and falling back into the quiver. Sugrīva was astonished! Overjoyed at having met the Lord, he fell devoutly at Rāma's feet."

“ ***Vālī and Sugrīva used to be very fond of each other, but circumstances destroyed that love. Such unforeseen circumstances can occur***

in our lives, too. Misunderstandings can sometimes change the course of our lives. We must try to understand the truth of the situation calmly. God's grace is necessary to face the misfortunes in life. Divine grace flows towards those who have innocent devotion.

30. Killing of Vālī

Grandmother sat in front of the lit lamp in the pūjā room, chanting her prayers. After some time, she continued with the story of Prince Rāma. Uṇṇi and Māḷu listened intently.

"Sugrīva rejoiced when he realized that Rāma had the strength to kill Vālī. That conviction filled him with devotion. Śrī Rāma embraced him and said, 'Sugrīva, go and challenge Vālī to a fight without any delay. I shall kill him and crown you King of Kiṣkindhā.'

"Sugrīva set out at once. When he reached the outskirts of the palace of Kiṣkindhā, he roared a challenge to Vālī. Trembling with uncontrolled anger, Vālī rushed out to kill Sugrīva. There ensured a prolonged fist battle between the two of them. They were both bathed in blood. Sugrīva was weakening rapidly as Vālī's blows rained down on him. They were so like each other that Rāma could not distinguish between them. Sugrīva retreated and came panting and exhausted to Śrī Rāma. He complained, 'Are You planning to get me killed by Vālī? I believed Your words, but now they seem to be in vain!'

"Śrī Rāma reassured the exhausted Sugrīva, 'Have no fear. Both of you, bathed in blood, looked alike to me and I could not distinguish the two of you. Here, let me adorn you with this flower garland. Wear it as you go back and challenge Vālī to fight you again.'

"After Śrī Rāma had put the flower garland around Sugrīva's neck, Sugrīva went again to the gates of the palace and challenged Vālī. The headstrong Vālī sprang up in anger, but was stopped by his wife, Tārā. She advised him, 'Do not take up the challenge. If Sugrīva, who ran away in defeat, has come back to challenge you again, be sure that a great warrior is on his side to support him."

"Vālī replied, 'When the enemy challenges me, I will not act like a coward and remain indoors. I have not harmed anyone. I have no other enemy. I shall finish off whoever has come prepared to kill me, and then return to you.'

"Tārā said, 'Our son Angada confided a secret to me today. The sons of Daśaratha, the brave princes Rāma and Lakṣmaṇa, are with Sugrīva. Someone abducted Śrī Rāma's wife. They came searching for Her to the Ṛṣyamukha mountain range and made a pact with Sugrīva. Śrī Rāma has promised Sugrīva to kill you and crown him king. In return, Sugrīva has promised to help Rāma search for and find Sītā. Angada heard this news through secret means. You cannot win a battle against Śrī Rāma. Therefore, make peace with Sugrīva.'

"Vālī said, 'Do not cry over me. I am aware that Śrī Rāma is the human incarnation of Lord Viṣṇu. Who in this world has more devotion to Rāma than me? Rāma is pure compassion towards His devotees. I am not scared of approaching Him.'

"Saying so, Vālī rushed out angrily to kill Sugrīva. It is difficult to describe the fierce fight that followed.

It was like a clash of titans! Sugrīva started to waver, weakening from Vālī's strong blows. From behind some trees, Śrī Rāma took out the *Indrāstra* weapon, aimed it at Vālī, and released it. It tore open the chest of Vālī, who collapsed with a huge roar. He was unconscious for some time. When he opened his eyes, he saw before him Lord Rāma and Lakṣmaṇa. With great displeasure and sadness, Vālī said, 'O Rāmacandra! Why did You attack me with an arrow shot while in hiding? What wrong have I done to You? Everyone says that You are a man of righteousness, great and noble. Why were You so cruel to me? I would have killed Rāvaṇa for You and brought back Sītā Dēvī safely.'

"Rāma replied, 'Your actions towards your brother have been base and ignoble. You have even made his wife your own. I am killing you to restore righteousness.'

"On hearing these stinging words, Vālī's heart and mind became pure. He felt as if Lord Viṣṇu Himself was standing before him, giving him darśan. With palms joined in devotion, Vālī said, 'Forgive my sins. Having Your darśan at the time of my death is a great blessing. Protect my son Angada. Please pull out this arrow, which is piercing my heart. Caress me and bestow Liberation on me.'

"With great love, Śrī Rāma pulled out the arrow piercing Vālī's chest and caressed him gently. With a sigh of pure bliss, Vālī closed his eyes and attained Liberation.

"When she learned about her husband's death, Tārā came running to the scene of his death and spoke words of anger and sorrow to Śrī Rāma. With great affection, the Lord made Tārā aware of the nature of the supreme self. Śrī Rāma spoke to Her about the principles of the individual self, the supreme self, the body, mind and intellect. This advice is known as *Tārōpadēśam*. When Tārā understood the nature of the universe, she became calm and peaceful.

"Afterwards, Śrī Rāma advised Angada to perform Vālī's cremation and funeral rites. After the funeral rites, He asked Lakṣmaṇa to crown Sugrīva King of Kiṣkindhā. The Lord did not enter Kiṣkindhā as He had pledged not to enter cities during His sojourn in the forest. He instructed Sugrīva, 'Proclaim Angada the crown prince. Rule the land as perfectly as your brother Vālī. Give me news of the whereabouts of Sītā within four months.'

"Acting on Śrī Rāma's instructions, Lakṣmaṇa crowned Sugrīva king."

Ignorance veils the inner light of the Self. Just as pure crystal reflects the colours around it, the pure self reflects the characteristics of ignorance. When man becomes established in the knowledge of the Self, he becomes pure and attains Liberation.

31. Dialogue between Hanumān and Sugrīva, Śrī Rāma's Grief

Uṇṇi came to the pūjā room, and sat down to pray with his grandmother while waiting for his mother. Māḷu came in after putting his baby sister, Śrīkuṭṭi, to sleep.

"After Sugrīva was crowned king of Kiṣkindhā, Lakṣmaṇa returned to Śrī Rāma. The two of them then journeyed to the peak of Mount Pravarṣaṇa. As they climbed up to the peak and surveyed the beauty below, they saw a golden cave. The surrounding area, which was wooded and green, had a golden aura. There was a crystalline purity to the atmosphere and the weather was pleasing. Śrī Rāma chose this pleasant spot to practise austerities for a four-month period.

"Living in this atmosphere, Lakṣmaṇa developed a longing to know how to attain mōkṣa through pūjā — ceremonial worship of the Lord. He prayed to Śrī Rāma to teach him, and the Lord instructed him on various ways to perform pūjā in order to attain mōkṣa. He also instructed Lakṣmaṇa on the universal principles underlying each aspect of pūjā. This part of the *Rāmāyaṇa* is called *Kriyamārgōpadēśam*.

"Uṇṇi, you are a small boy now. When you grow up and want to understand the secrets of this vast universe and the ultimate reality, you must read the *Rāmāyaṇa*."

Uṇṇi nodded, "Yes, Grandma."

Grandma continued, "Śrī Rāma's instructions to Tārā and Lakṣmaṇa on universal principles, the supreme self, and how to merge with It reveal Him to be a divine incarnation. The tragic incidents in His life reveal Rāma's humanity — His compassion, sensitivity and consideration for others. While speaking to Lakṣmaṇa on spiritual principles, the sudden memory of Sītā would overwhelm Rāma, causing Him to cry inconsolably from grief and longing. Rāma spent much time on the mountain peak yearning for Sītā.

"Now let us take a look at what is happening in Kiṣkindhā. Sugrīva was over-indulging in the pleasures available to a king. He seemed to have forgotten the pact he made with Śrī Rāma. Hanumān understood this. One day, when no one else was around, he approached his king, bowed before him, and said, 'O King! Listen carefully to what I am going to say. Have you forgotten the pact you made with Śrī Rāmacandra? He has honoured the treaty in every way. You are now King of Kiṣkindhā. I feel that you do not remember His act with gratitude. Those who forget the people who help them are like living corpses. Śrī Rāma will be waiting for you. The time period He gave you is almost over. You are lolling around, drunk. Remember, the arrow that killed Vālī is still in Śrī Rāmacandra's hands!'

"Sugrīva suddenly felt afraid when he heard the dire warnings from Hanumān. He also felt remorseful for having forgotten the Lord and His mission. He said, 'O Vāyuputra, I am blessed to have ministers like you, who advise me on the right path. Send a message immediately to the seven islands, and ask all the brave monkeys to assemble here. Those who disobey my orders will be summarily executed. This is my command!' Hanumān did as commanded.

"At the same time, Śrī Rāma felt the days dragging on as He grieved over Sītā. He told Lakṣmaṇa, 'We don't know who carried Sītā away and to where. Sugrīva seems to have forgotten us, indulging himself in the lap of luxury. My four months of austerities are over. Sugrīva has not even started his search. I feel that he will soon be headed where his brother went!'

"Lakṣmaṇa, who was hot-tempered, could no longer control the anger that had been simmering inside him. He sprang up, saying, 'I'm going to finish Sugrīva off!'

"Rāma restrained him, saying, 'Do not kill him. Just see to it that he becomes really frightened! Just remind him, "The time has come for you to go on the same journey as Vālī." We can consider our options after hearing what he says.'

"In response to his brother's order, Lakṣmaṇa strode down the mountains, came to Sugrīva's palace, and twanged his bow. Hearing it, the monkeys quaked in terror and started running helter-skelter. Angada and Hanumān made their way hastily to Lakṣmaṇa and bowed devoutly before him. They invited him into the palace. Seeing their cordial reception, Lakṣmaṇa felt his anger cooling down. Tārā told him, 'Do not be mad with

Sugrīva. In response to his command, the monkey armies are arriving in Kiṣkindhā.'

"Lakṣmaṇa met Sugrīva and berated him, 'Why did you forget my brother, Śrī Rāmacandra? The arrow that killed Vālī is still with Rāma!'

"Filled with remorse, Sugrīva got up from his throne and bowed down before Lakṣmaṇa. Hanumān explained, "Sugrīva has not forgotten Śrī Rāma. He has made preparations to search for Sītā. The monkey armies have reached here from far and wide. It will not be long before we achieve success.'

"With humility and devotion, Sugrīva asked Lakṣmaṇa to sit down and then worshipped him. He also sang the praises of Śrī Rāma.

"When he heard the words of a repentant Sugrīva, Lakṣmaṇa's anger evaporated. He said, 'I was enraged by your indolence. That is why I spoke in anger. Forgive me my harsh words. Let us go at once to my brother Rāma. He is alone on the mountain peak.'

"'Yes, let us start our journey immediately,' said Sugrīva, who at once made preparations for their journey to meet Śrī Rāma."

“ ***To err is human. Even if you occupy an exalted position, you must beg forgiveness from even the lowliest if you do wrong. We***

must also develop a heart that is expansive enough to forgive the mistakes of others.

32. Story of Svayamprabhā

The oil lamp was lit in the pūjā room. Grandmother continued with the narration of the *Rāmāyaṇa*.

"Lakṣmaṇa and the band of monkeys — including King Sugrīva, Hanumān, Angada and Nīla — set out to meet Śrī Rāma. After travelling for a long time, they saw Him sitting at the mouth of a cave. Even though the separation from Sītā was a torment for the Lord, He graciously smiled at Sugrīva, hugged him and made him sit near Him. He said, 'Hope you're fine.'

"Sugrīva's heart overflowed with joy. Pointing to the army of monkeys, he said, 'My Lord, these are brave and skilled monkeys ready to do Your bidding.' He explained to Rāma the strength and capabilities of each commander. He pointed out strong Jāmbavān, the commander in chief of his monkey army, and Hanumān, his brilliant prime minister. 'Command us, my Lord! We have come prepared for anything!'

"The Lord said, 'Sugrīva, think through things, make the right decisions, and act upon them!'

"In obedience to Rāma's instructions, Sugrīva sent his army in all directions. Each division had a hundred thousand monkeys. He said, 'Come back within 30 days with information on the whereabouts of Sītā Dēvī. Those who delay will be executed!'

"The various divisions set off on their holy search. Hanumān approached Rāma, and stood before Him with palms joined worshipfully. Rāma took off the ring gifted to him by the sages, gave it to Hanumān, and said, 'Vāyuputra, put this ring, which has my name carved on it, in Sītā's hand. This way, you can earn Her trust. You are the only one capable of accomplishing this mission.' He also communicated to Hanumān a sentence that only Sītā and He knew, so that Sītā would be convinced that Hanumān was Rāma's messenger.

"Under Jāmbavān's and Nīla's leadership, the monkey army set out to the south, which was where Rāvaṇa's kingdom was located. They searched all the mountains and towns along the way until they reached the thick forest of the Vindhya mountain ranges. They mistook a rākṣasa roaming there, attacking wild animals and eating them alive, for Rāvaṇa, and killed him. When they realized their mistake, they resumed their search. They entered a dark forest. Their lips, tongue and mouth were parched with thirst. There was no water to be found anywhere."

Uṇṇi said, "How horrible! Weren't there any ponds or streams inside the forest?"

"No Uṇṇi, they searched everywhere but could not find even a small rivulet."

"What happened then?"

"By the grace of God, they were able to discover a cave. The entrance to the cave was partially hidden by creepers. The monkeys noticed birds flying out of the cave; the wings of the birds were dripping with water. This was a sure sign that there was water inside the cave. Under Hanumān's leadership, the monkeys entered the cave. As it was pitch dark inside, they could not see each other, and became frightened, not knowing the way in or the way out. The monkeys decided to hold hands and slowly walked forward in a single file. After inching their way ahead in the dark for a long way, they suddenly saw light far ahead. They walked on and reached a place that was beautiful beyond belief. There were ponds sparkling like jewels, trees laden with fruits, and homes in which delicious honey and food had been prepared and kept ready. Astonished, the monkeys kept on moving forward. They came upon a radiant woman, a sage, who was meditating on a golden throne inlaid with jewels. The monkeys prostrated before the saint. With great happiness, she asked them, 'Who are you? Why did you come here? Who guided you inside? Where are you going?'

"Hanumān humbly bowed down before the radiant woman and told her the story of Rāma, and that they were a 100,000-strong monkey army travelling south in search of Sītā. They were parched with thirst and had wandered into the cave in search of precious water. Hanumān then humbly asked, 'Please tell us who you are. We would like to know.'

"When she heard about Rāma, about whom Hanumān had spoken with utmost devotion, her face became bright with happiness. She said, 'O monkeys, eat your fill of the fruits and drink your fill of the clear water. Come back to me having appeased your thirst and hunger. Then I shall tell you about myself.'

"The monkeys tucked into the fruits, drank the water, finished the honey, and came back content. They bowed before the radiant sage, who started to tell Hanumān about herself. 'Viśvakarma, the celestial architect, had a beautiful daughter named Hēmā, who was a gifted dancer. Pleased with her dancing skills, Lord Śiva bestowed on her this beautiful home. Hēmā lived here happily for eons, after which she merged into God. I am her companion, Svayamprabhā. I am the daughter of a *gandharva* (celestial being) and a devotee of Viṣṇu. Hēmā advised me to remain here. She revealed that Lord Viṣṇu would incarnate as Śrī Rāma in the Trētā Yuga; that an army of monkeys would come here in search of Sītā Dēvī; and that I should prepare a feast for them and a place for them to rest and refresh themselves. After hosting you, Hēmā advised me to go and attain mōkṣa in the holy presence of Śrī Rāma. I have been waiting here for you for many centuries, absorbed in chanting the sacred name of Śrī Rāma. Please close your eyes. I shall transport you to the right path. Thereafter, I shall go and have the darśan of Lord Rāma!'

"The monkeys stood still and closed their eyes. With her yogic powers, Svayamprabhā teleported them to the forest and showed them the right path. She travelled to where Śrī Rāma was sitting with Lakṣmaṇa and Sugrīva. She bowed down before her Lord, sang His praises, and circumambulated him reverentially. The hymn glorifying the Lord is known as the *'Svayamprabhā stuti'* in the *Rāmāyaṇa*. She prostrated again and again to the Lord. Śrī Rāma blessed her and advised her to retire to the Badaryāśram and meditate upon Him. Svayamprabhā spent the rest of her life as an ascetic there, and finally merged into the sacred feet of Lord Nārāyaṇa."

> ***Those who have gained divine knowledge through devotion for the Lord will know the past and future.***

33. Angada's Doubts, Sampāti's Words

Grandma was waiting for Uṇṇi and Māḷu in the pūjā room. The oil lamp cast a serene glow on the pictures of the deities. After Māḷu and Uṇṇi had settled down and said their prayers, Grandma resumed narrating the story of Prince Rāma.

"The monkeys started searching the forest, in vain, for any sign of Sītā Dēvī. Angada became anxious and despondent. He addressed the other monkeys, 'My dear friends, we do not know how many days we spent in the enchanted cave of Svayamprabhā Dēvī. Sugrīva has said that if we do not get back with news of Sītā Dēvī in a month, he will kill us. I'm sure that the one month is long over. Therefore, I am not going any further. I shall end my life here itself. You may return.'

"Other monkeys said, 'Let's return to that cave, which is like heaven. Nobody will find us there. We can live in great comfort!'

"Hanumān, who was listening to their disheartened talk, said, 'Angada, why do you harbour such negative thoughts? Śrī Rāma has great affection for you. He knows how capable you are. Do not heed the opinions of these foolish monkeys. What makes you think no one will know you're hiding inside a cave? Is there any place in this universe that Rāma's arrows cannot reach? Let me share a secret with you. Śrī Rāma is the incarnation of Lord Viṣṇu. He was born to obliterate the rākṣasas.

We were born to serve Him. Therefore, cast away your despair and continue leading our efforts.'

"Hearing Hanumān's words, Angada became calm. The monkeys combed the Vindhya ranges, looking for some sign of Rāma's consort, in vain. Finally they reached the Mahēndra mountains. From the peak, one could see the ocean stretching away to the south. They did not know the way forward. There was only the ocean in front of them. The monkeys were disappointed and dispirited. All their hopes died. They had long exceeded the time limit that Sugrīva set. The monkeys decided to end their lives rather than die at the hands of Sugrīva. Spreading darbha grass on the sand, the monkeys lay down to die."

Uṇṇi said, "That's terrible, Grandma! The poor monkeys! What happened to them?"

Grandmother said, "When the monkeys had laid down, a huge old vulture emerged slowly from a cave in the Mahēndra mountains. Looking at the monkeys, he said happily, 'I was starving. I have become old and weak and have no wings to fly and catch my prey. God has brought me food right in front of me. I can eat the monkeys when they die!'

"The vulture's words unnerved the monkeys. They began lamenting to one other, 'How sad! This horrible old vulture will tear us apart and gobble us up, one by one. We have failed Śrī Rāma, and we seem fated to die at the cruel beak of this bird. We must be great sinners.

Look at how blessed Jaṭāyu was. He died fighting for Śrī Rāma and attained salvation.'

"The old bird was listening keenly to the conversation of the monkeys. He suddenly interrupted them and asked, 'Who are you? The name of Jaṭāyu is nectar to my ears. Who are you? Come near me. Do not be afraid.'

"Angada meditated upon Śrī Rāma and then calmly went up to the old vulture. He told him who they were and what their quest was. He described how Rāvaṇa had severed Jaṭāyu's wings with the candrahāsa sword. He spoke about how Jaṭāyu had lain patiently, waiting for Rāma to come so that he could tell the Lord who had abducted Sītā. He described how Śrī Rāma, the gentle and compassionate prince, had taken the avian king's head and chest on His lap and caressed him until his soul attained salvation. 'Now, please tell us about yourself,' said Angada.

"The huge bird said, 'I am Sampāti. Jaṭāyu was my younger brother. Alas, he died before me! Let me perform his last rites. Please carry me to the shore of the ocean.'

"The monkeys lifted Sampāti up and carried him to the shore. After he had performed the last rites, the monkeys carried him back to his cave and placed him down gently. Pleased with their service, Sampāti said, 'There is a mountain named Trikuṭa in the ocean. On top of that mountain lies the land of Lanka, which is where Rāvaṇa's kingdom is located. Sītā Dēvī dwells there, under a tree in the grove of Aśōka trees. One of you must jump across the ocean and go to Lanka. You will be able to see Sītā. Once you have made sure of Her whereabouts, go back at once to Śrī Rāmacandra and give Him the news. Śrī Rāma has the strength to kill Rāvaṇa. The rākṣasa who killed my brother must be destroyed!'

"Sampāti then recounted the history of his early life to the monkeys. A long time ago, Sampāti and his younger brother had raced each other up into the skies, to test their strength and swiftness. When they came near the sun, the heat caused Jaṭāyu's wings to smoulder and burn. Sampāti saved his brother's wings by shielding them with his own. As a result, Sampāti's wings became charred and he fell to the ground, a wingless bird. Jaṭāyu also fell to the ground, but his wings were safe. For three days, Sampāti remained unconscious. When he regained consciousness, he did not know where Jaṭāyu was. As his wings were charred, Sampāti could not fly in search of his brother. He dragged himself to the āśram of Sage Niśākaran. Seeing the bird's pitiable condition, the saint felt compassion towards him. He gave the bird knowledge of the supreme self and the reasons for birth, death, merit, demerits, the cycle of birth and death, and other such recondite matters. He also told him, "During the Trētā Yuga, you will meet the monkeys who are searching for Sītā. You can share with them the knowledge of

Sītā and Her captor. At that point in time, you will grow new wings!'

"Amazingly, Sampāti began to sprout big and strong wings. As he soared into the skies, he blessed the monkey army: 'O fortunate monkeys, may all good come to you! You can cross the oceans with the constant remembrance of the Lord!'"

> ***Unshakeable faith in the Lord will take one to the heights of success. The obstacles on the way will vanish, like unravelled knots.***

34. Planning for a Sea Crossing

Uṇṇi said, "Grandma, the stories from the *Rāmāyaṇa* are so exciting. Sampāti has grown new wings! What happened to the monkeys?"

Mother and grandmother stole glances at each other and smiled at Uṇṇi's eager anticipation. Grandma said, "The monkeys watched in growing astonishment as Sampāti sprouted wings that instantly became big and strong. They gazed at the huge bird as it disappeared into the sky. Then, they held a meeting to decide how to cross the ocean. Gazing at the vast ocean, they beheld a vast expanse of water shimmering in front of them. Surely there were crocodiles and other dangerous creatures lurking beneath! They scanned the horizon but were unable to see beyond. Their hearts grew heavy. They said, 'How can we ever cross this great ocean? It is impossible! We can't even see the other side. Death is certain if we attempt to cross it!' They huddled together, murmuring to each other.

"Hearing their talk, Angada said, 'O great monkeys! You're all brave and strong. Think carefully. Whoever decides that he has the strength and ability to cross the ocean will save all our lives and ease Rāma and Lakṣmaṇa's pain.'

"The monkeys looked at each other and remained silent. Nobody volunteered for this dangerous task that was well-nigh impossible. Angada said, 'O monkeys! Do come forward and enumerate to me your strengths and abilities.'

"Each monkey came forward to declare his abilities. One monkey said, 'I can leap 80 miles, or 10 *yōjanas*.'"

Uṇṇi asked, "What's a yōjana, Grandma?"

"It's a unit for measuring distance, like kilometre," said Grandma.

Uṇṇi nodded his head. Grandma continued, "In this manner, one by one, the monkeys started to enumerate their abilities. The monkeys variously said they could leap 20, 30 and 60 yōjanas. There was none who claimed to be able to leap more than 60 yōjanas. The sea was at least a hundred yōjanas wide. Jāmbavān, who had been listening to the monkeys, said, 'It seems that none among you are capable of leaping across the sea. Alas, I have grown old! I had many abilities when I was young. When Viṣṇu incarnated as Vāmana and covered the earth in three steps, I had beaten my great drum and circumambulated His cosmic form in 10 minutes, but now, I am unable to leap across even this sea.'

"Hearing this, Angada said, 'I can cross the sea in one stride, but will not be able to return likewise.'

"Jāmbavān replied, 'O Prince Angada, even if you were ready to leap across the ocean, we would not let you. There is one among your servants who is capable of this feat, impossible to everyone else.'

"Miffed by Jāmbavān's words, Angada said, 'But they have already said that they are incapable of doing so. It's better that we fast unto death!'

"As this talk was going on, one among the monkeys was sitting to a side, lost in thought. Do you know who it was, Uṇṇi? It was Hanumān. Jāmbavān looked at Hanumān and said, 'Hey, Hanumān! Why are you so silent? I've no doubt that you're the best person for this job. You are a partial manifestation of Lord Śiva and son of Vāyu, the wind. You are a *sattvic* soul, pure and energetic. I have heard how, right after you were born, you mistook the sun for a fruit and jumped up 500 feet to pluck and eat the ripe red fruit. You were felled by the *Vajrāyudha,* Indra's thunderbolt, which caused a wound in your chin bone called the "hanu;" hence your name. As you fell to the earth, your father, the wind god, caught you and took you to the netherworld. The creatures on earth and in the heavens began suffocating owing to a lack of air movement. The Trinity and dēvas went to the underworld to propitiate your father with many boons. You were granted the boon of eternal life. You are a *cirañjīvi,* an immortal. You will definitely be able to cross the vast ocean. Not only that, Śrī Rāma entrusted his jewelled ring to you. Think about why He did so, why He put so much faith in you. It's not right that you, who have such superhuman powers, should sit quietly like this!'

"Jāmbavān listed the abilities of Hanumān. Hanumān became happy and confident. His mind became strong. He grew in size until he resembled a mountain. Roaring like a lion, Hanumān said, 'I shall leap across this ocean without any effort. After rescuing Sītā Dēvī, I shall burn Lanka to ashes. Or, I shall imprison Rāvaṇa, hold him in my left hand, and, with my right, rip out the Trikuṭa Mountain with Lanka on its crest. I shall then offer both at the feet of Lord Rāmacandra!'"

Uṇṇi's eyes had grown large. Without being aware of it, he was repeatedly uttering "Wow!" in excitement. It was as if he was seeing Hanumān right in front of him. Seeing the expression on his face, Uṇṇi's grandmother and mother smiled.

Grandma continued, "Hearing Hanumān's words, Jāmbavān joyfully said, 'O Vāyuputra! It is enough if you convey Rāmacandra's message to Sītā. Return after your mission has been successfully completed. The Lord will decide what should be done afterwards. You can display your great valour during the war with Rāvaṇa. Go now! May no obstacle mar your journey!'

"The monkey army gave Hanumān a warm send-off. Hanumān climbed up to the peak of the Mahēndra mountains. There he stood, glowing like Garuda."

"*One might not know of the talents hidden within oneself. But if others have identified*

them, they must convince him of his potential and boost his confidence so that he may act. Parents can spot their children's talents; teachers, their students'; and friends, their friends'.

35. Crossing the Ocean, Encountering Obstacles

Grandmother continued with her narration. "Hanumān meditated upon Śrī Rāma and prayed for strength to leap across the ocean, a hundred yōjanas wide. Looking at the assembled monkeys, he said, 'Friends, I am fully prepared. With Śrī Rāmacandra's blessings, I shall fly through the sky and cross the ocean in one great leap. I shall reach Lanka, have Sītā Dēvī's darśan, leap back again, and inform Śrī Rāmacandra about my darśan today itself. As the Lord resides in my heart, I will not meet any obstacle on the way!'

"Hanumān spread his hands out wide and lifted his tail up high. He raised his head, bent his knees a little, braced himself and leapt into the sky. The monkeys gazed at him until he became a small speck and finally disappeared like an eagle into space."

Uṇṇi's face lit up with happiness and enjoyment. He laughed excitedly, seeing before him the mighty leap of Hanumān, son of the Wind God. Grandma and Māḷu laughed to see the small boy's happiness.

Grandma continued, "Seeing Hanumān flying through the skies, the dēvas decided to test him. They sent, Surasā, mother of serpents, to stop his passage through the air."

Uṇṇi was upset. "Why did they do that, Grandma?"

"To test his strength and capacity. Surasā appeared in front of Hanumān, and roared at him. 'Hey monkey! I eat all the creatures who pass this way fearlessly. Get inside my mouth. I'm very hungry and I've no time to waste!'

"Hanumān replied, 'O Goddess! I am travelling to Lanka at Śrī Rāma's behest, in search of Sītā. Let me meet Sītā Dēvī and inform Lord Rāma of my darśan. I shall then return to you, and you can gobble me up. This is my promise!'

"But Surasā was not willing to let him go. She said, 'Hey monkey! I'm hungry and thirsty. I'm unable to contain my hunger.'

"'If that is so, please open your mouth, replied Hanumān, and he increased his girth to a yōjana. Surasā at once opened her mouth until it was five yōjanas wide. As soon as Hanumān increased his size, Surasā would proportionately increase the size of her mouth, to swallow Hanumān. When Surasā had made her mouth a gaping hole of fifty yōjanas in diameter, Hanumān suddenly shrank his body to the size of a thumb, entered Surasā's mouth and then darted out immediately. He then said, 'O Dēvī! Prostrations to you!'

"Surasā was pleased. She said, 'O Vāyuputra, the dēvas sent me to test your strength and skill. You will succeed in your mission. Delay not, but go forth speedily to Sītā Dēvī, and inform Her Lord after you meet Her.'

"Hanumān continued his journey. It was then that the sea commanded the flying Mount Maināka, 'O Maināka, rise up and stand tall so that Hanumān can rest on you!'

"Stretching itself out of the ocean, Maināka addressed Hanumān, 'O Vāyuputra! You must be tired from the long leap. Rest on me. Refresh yourself with some fruit and water.'

"Hanumān replied, "No, thank you. I am going on a mission for Rāma. I have no time to rest and refresh myself. Nevertheless, thank you for your gracious invitation.' Saying so, he patted Maināka affectionately and flew on. Then there arose before him another obstacle."

"What was that, Grandma?" Uṇṇi was beside himself with anxiety. His little heart was longing for Sītā Dēvī to be comforted by the sight of Hanumān, the messenger of Śrī Rāma.

"There was a rākṣasī called Simhikā who lived inside the ocean and who would seize shadows. She caught hold of Hanumān's shadow and thus arrested his flight. When Hanumān looked down to see who was clinging on to his shadow and preventing him from flying on, he saw a fat rākṣasī down below. He gave her one kick, and thus despatched Simhikā.

"He flew on swiftly and saw the spires of Lanka as the sun was setting. Hanumān was astounded by the beauty of Lanka. The city walls were made of gold. Huge moats beneath the walls made it difficult to enter the city. He decided to meditate on the Lord, and to enter the city secretly at night. Making his body as tiny as a mustard seed, he tried to pass through the city gates silently, but the city's guardian, Lanka Lakṣmī, appeared before him in the guise of a rākṣasī. 'Hey fool!' she roared. 'You cannot enter the city without my permission!' She tried to punch Hanumān, who ducked, then clenched his fist and punched the rākṣasī. Lanka Lakṣmī fell and began vomiting blood. After some time, she stood up and said, 'I have been guarding this city for eons. Brahmā, the Creator, had promised me that I would be freed from my curse during the Trētā Yuga, when Hanumān, Śrī Rāma's messenger, comes in search of Sītā Dēvī and punches me. You may enter. I am no longer enslaved. I am departing from Lanka. Sītā Dēvī is sitting under the Śimśapa tree in the Aśōka Grove, and pining for Her Lord. She is surrounded and guarded by rākṣasīs. Go and meet her at once, and inform the Lord without delay. May your endeavour be crowned with success!' Saying so, Lanka Lakṣmī disappeared.

"Tomorrow, Uṇṇi, I shall tell you about Hanumān's darśan of Sītā." Grandmother kissed Uṇṇi on his cheek.

> ***On the journey towards our goal, we will encounter many obstacles and temptations. Face the obstacles with courage and self-confidence, and overlook the temptations. Maintain remembrance of God.***

36. Sighting of Sītā, Approach of Rāvaṇa

Grandma spent some time meditating on Śrī Rāma. She then continued with the narration of the *Rāmāyaṇa*. "Lanka Lakṣmī blessed Hanumān and disappeared."

Māḷu asked, "Mother, there is an inner meaning to this, isn't there? When you say that Lanka Lakṣmī disappeared, doesn't it also mean that the Goddess of Auspiciousness and Prosperity disappeared from Lanka?"

"Yes, Māḷu," said Grandma, "Very true! Bad times had started for Rāvaṇa. As soon as Lanka Lakṣmī disappeared, Hanumān shrank in size and entered the city. It is said that the moment Hanumān set foot inside the city, Sītā's and Rāvaṇa's left side started quivering, while Śrī Rāma's right side started quivering. When the left side quivers for a woman, it is a sign of impending goodness. For men, it is the quivering of the right side that heralds good fortune. The quivering of Rāvaṇa's left side was a bad omen for the rākṣasa king. Hanumān went all around the city, searching for Sītā Dēvī. Suddenly, recalling Lanka Lakṣmī's words, he entered the grove of Aśōka trees. Bearing the gentle fragrance of flowers, his father, the wind god, accompanied Hanumān and took him to the Śimśapa tree. Lo and behold! There sat Sītā Dēvī. Her hair was in disarray. Her clothes were dishevelled. He body had become thin with the grief of parting from Her dearest Rāma. She was sitting like a drooping flower, Her divinity a gentle aura around Her, the Rāma-nāma constantly on Her lips. Rākṣasīs surrounded her.

"Hanumān hid under the leaves of the tree. His heart went out to Sītā. It was then that Rāvaṇa came to visit Her.

"Uṇṇi, deep within him, Rāvaṇa knew that he would die at the hands of Śrī Rāma for his unpardonable crime. But his mind was full of enmity towards the Lord. Yet, he knew that being killed by Śrī Rāma would grant him Liberation. The mind of Rāvaṇa was filled with cruel thoughts.

"Seeing Rāvaṇa, Sītā became frightened. She sat still, with downcast face, looking withdrawn. Hanumān remained seated where he was, a silent witness. Rāvaṇa spoke to Sītā with great humility. 'O lovely lady, why do You spend Your time grieving? Consider me, the emperor of this country, Your servant. Please raise Your head and look into my face. I am by far a better choice than Your husband. Rāma is weak and helpless. He lacks the strength to cross the ocean and carry You back with Him. You, the most beautiful of princesses, should not waste Your life grieving for a forest hermit. He is in no way suited to You. Accept me as Your husband, and I shall make You my empress. You shall live in the lap of luxury, and I shall gratify every small desire of Yours.'

"Sītā felt rage seething within Her. Plucking out a blade of grass, She glared at Rāvaṇa, knowing that he was intelligent enough to understand the meaning of Her action — that, for Her, he was only as insignificant as a blade of grass. She said as much, 'Hey, cruel one! To me, you are only as important and significant as this blade of grass. If you were just and noble, you would not have disguised yourself as a sage and carried me away. My husband will definitely cross this ocean and reach Lanka. Rāma's arrows will pierce your heart. Know that my Raghu Rāma is the incarnation of Lord Viṣṇu, born to destroy you. He will kill you and all the other cruel rākṣasas, and take me back with Him!'

"Incensed by Her words, Rāvaṇa unsheathed his sword to kill Sītā but was stopped by his wife, Maṇḍōdarī. Gripping his hand tightly, she said, 'Do not kill a woman, O Lord of Lanka. Refrain from this sinful action.'

"Rāvaṇa obeyed the wise words of his wife. But his desire for Sītā grew. He ordered the rākṣasīs guarding Sītā to kindle love for him within Her by beguiling Her with sweet words.

"After Rāvaṇa's departure, the rākṣasīs continued to torment Sītā with harsh words. Finding their taunts unbearable, Sītā remained forlorn and heartsick under the tree. There was a rākṣasī named Trijaṭā guarding Sītā. She was the daughter of Vibhīṣaṇa, younger brother of Rāvaṇa. Vibhīṣaṇa was a great devotee of Śrī Rāma. Trijaṭā was also just, noble and righteous in her conduct. She ordered the other rākṣasīs to stop hurting Sītā with harsh words. Trijaṭā said, 'Hey rākṣasīs, prostrate in front of Dēvī Sītā! I had a vivid dream yesterday. I dreamt that Rāma and Lakṣmaṇa reached Lanka and that they destroyed Rāvaṇa and his evil army. They crowned Vibhīṣaṇa king and carried Sītā safely back with them to Ayōdhyā. This was my dream, which will come true. Therefore, let us not harm Dēvī.'

"When they heard this, the rākṣasīs became afraid. After some time, they went to sleep."

> ***Even when they know the truth, some people are slaves to sensual pleasure, and conveniently ignore reality. They behave foolishly. Rāvaṇa was one such person.***

37. Dialogue between Hanumān and Sītā

When Uṇṇi and Māḷu entered the pūjā room, they saw that Grandma had adorned Śrī Rāma's picture with a garland and lit the oil lamp.

Uṇṇi asked, "Grandma, did Hanumān talk to Sītā? Was Sītā relieved?"

Continuing with her narration of the *Rāmāyaṇa*, Grandma said, "All the rākṣasīs fell asleep but sleep eluded Sītā. She was lonely and frightened. You cannot fall asleep if you are scared and sad. In sorrow, Sītā said, 'In this land, I have no one to call my own. In the morning, the rākṣasīs will eat me. My Lord must have forgotten me. It is better to die than to continue living in this manner.' Thus Sītā lamented, sitting forlorn under the Śimśapa tree.

"Hanumān who had been secretly watching the recent events unfolding heard Sītā's heartbroken lament and thought, 'It is time for me to act!' In a voice that only Sītā could hear, Hanumān narrated the story of Śrī Rāma. He narrated the events from the time of His divine birth and that of his brothers until the point where Hanumān reached the Śimśapa as Rāma's messenger. He did not omit a single event. Finally, he ended his narration with the following words, spoken with great emotion, 'I am indeed blessed to be able to see Dēvī underneath this Śimśapa tree! My humble greetings to You!'

"When She heard about Rāma and His celebrated exploits, Sītā's joy was boundless. But She did not trust

Herself fully. She said to Herself, 'Did I really hear the story of Rāma from the skies above? Or was it just a fancy of my mind? No, I really did hear the narration of Rāma's glories. But who narrated it?' Looking around suspiciously, Sītā said, 'Whoever it is, please come before me.'

"Hanumān made himself very small as he jumped nimbly down from the tree and stood before Sītā. Suddenly, fear rippled through Sītā's heart. Could this be another of Rāvaṇa's vile tricks? Sītā kept Her head down. Hanumān understood Her fear and gently said, 'Dēvī, please trust me. I have not come in disguise. I am a messenger of Śrī Rāma, the servant of Sugrīva, and the son of Vāyu.'

"Sītā was relieved to hear Hanumān's answer. In great joy, She asked him to narrate Rāma's story again. Hanumān told Sītā about how Rāma and Lakṣmaṇa had been wandering from forest to forest in search of Her. He also told Her about the pact between Sugrīva and Rāma. Then to prove his bona fides and to make Sītā happier, he presented to Her Rāma's ring and whispered the secret word that Rāma had asked him to tell Sītā. When Sītā saw Rāma's ring, in which was engraved his holy name, tears of ecstatic joy streamed down Her cheeks. Bringing the ring to Her forehead, She held it there reverentially. She blessed Hanumān and said, 'You have given my life back to me. You are truly a blessed soul and a worthy devotee of Rāma. Please inform my Lord of my suffering in this place. Tell Him to come here within two months and free me from my misery. He must kill Rāvaṇa and save me!'

"Hearing this, Hanumān consoled Sītā Dēvī. 'Mother, I shall inform Lord Rāma immediately of all that You have told me and of all that I saw. Lord Rāma will come to You with Lakṣmaṇa and the army of monkeys, kill Rāvaṇa, and carry You safely back to Ayōdhyā. Have no doubt about it.'

"Sītā asked him, 'How? How will they cross the ocean to get here?'

"Hanumān said, 'We will find a way. If not, I will carry Śrī Rāma, Lakṣmaṇa and the monkey army on my shoulders and carry them over to Lanka. Please give me a memento for the Lord to trust my words, and please tell me a special word.'

"When She heard this, Sītā thought for a while. Then She took out the crest jewel that Rāma had once given Her, and which She had hidden in Her thick hair. Handing it to Hanumān, She said, 'When we were living in Citrakūṭa, Jayanta, son of Indra, assumed the form of a crow and stole the pieces of meat I was drying. When I flicked small stones at it, the crow pecked me with its sharp beak and scratched me with its talons. Seeing this, my husband became enraged. He plucked a blade of grass, chanted a mantra, and hurled the blade of grass at the crow. The scared crow, knowing that all was lost, fell at my husband's feet. The blade of grass blinded one of his eyes, but otherwise, Jayanta was allowed to go free. Please convey this story to Rāma.'

"Having received the crest jewel and message from Sītā, Hanumān prepared to leave. When he sought permission to leave, Sītā Dēvī asked, 'Son, are you monkeys all so small? How will you win the battle against the rākṣasas, who are as big and strong as mountains?'

"Revealing to Her his mountainous size, Hanumān reassured Sītā. 'All the monkeys are as big as I!'

"Pleased, Sītā said, 'Son, you may leave. Place the crest jewel today itself at my Lord's feet. Convey all my sorrows to Him. May no obstacle come your way!'

"Hanumān circumambulated Sītā Dēvī with great devotion and set out on his return journey."

> **"*The messenger must always be sincere and steadfast in his mission. There should be no blemish or impurity in his mission. The words of the master should flow unobstructed through the messenger. Hanumān is a perfect messenger.***

38. Lashing of Lanka

Uṇṇi and his mother were listening intently to the narration of the *Rāmāyaṇa*. Grandma continued, "Hanumān bid farewell to Sītā Dēvī, his heart gladdened by Her blessing. Then he climbed up the distant branch of a tree and thought, 'I have accomplished what I came for. But, as a messenger, I have one more job to finish. Shouldn't I let Rāvaṇa know of my arrival? How can I achieve this?' Hanumān thought for some time. Then he started wreaking havoc in the garden. He did not touch the surroundings of the tree under which Sītā was sitting. But he uprooted and tore apart all the other plants, tree branches and creepers in the garden."

Uṇṇi laughed. "What happened then? Did Rāvaṇa get to hear about it?"

Grandma continued, "Hearing the sounds of trees being uprooted and potted plants crashing to the ground, the rākṣasīs started in shock. By then Hanumān had already killed many of the guards. Sītā remained seated, acting as if She knew nothing. The rākṣasīs ran to Rāvaṇa and told him, 'O Lord, a terrible creature as big as a mountain has destroyed the beautiful garden. He has killed the guards and is now busy destroying the houses in the garden. He is not afraid of anyone but we are frightened of him!'

"Rāvaṇa trembled in anger. He sent 100,000 rākṣasa soldiers to wage war upon Hanumān. Hanumān roared and they fell unconscious. He killed them all with a thorn branch. Rāvaṇa was beside himself with rage. He sent five more battalions headed by their commanders. They also met with the same fate. The sons of ministers and other divisions of armies confronted Hanumān. Hanumān had by then got hold of an iron pestle, with which he killed them all.

"Rāvaṇa's anger now turned into fear and sorrow. The son of Rāvaṇa, Akṣay Kumār, promised his father that he would imprison Hanumān and bring him to his father. Akṣay Kumār wounded Hanumān with his arrows but eventually died at Hanumān's hands. Rāvaṇa became sad. He summoned his eldest son, Mēghanād, who had conquered Indra and was hence also called Indrajit. The son consoled his father, and vowed to bring the monkey back as a prisoner, come what may.

"He went to war with an impressive arsenal of weapons. A fierce war erupted between the two of them. Indrajit's arrows wounded Hanumān on his head, chest, legs and tail. Hanumān killed Indrajit's charioteer with the thorn branch, and then crushed the chariot and the horses. Finally, Indrajit used the *Brahmāstra.*[12] Out of respect for and devotion to Lord Brahmā, Hanumān did not counter the arrow, but feigned unconsciousness and fell to the ground.

"Indrajit then bound Hanumān and dragged him back to Rāvaṇa's court. Bowing down before his father,

12 Supernatural weapon.

Indrajit said, 'I have brought before you this monkey, who killed thousands of rākṣasas, but was eventually defeated and imprisoned by the Brahmāstra. Nevertheless, he is no ordinary monkey.'

"Rāvaṇa commanded his minister, Prahasta, to find out everything he could about Hanumān. Prahasta calmly questioned Hanumān, 'Hey monkey! Who are you? Who sent you here? Why did you destroy our beautiful garden? Why did you kill all these rākṣasas. Speak without fear. You will be treated justly in Rāvaṇa's court.'

"Hanumān meditated upon the form of Śrī Rāmacandra. Then, gazing at Rāvaṇa, he replied. 'I am the messenger of Śrī Rāmacandra. When He was living in the forest with His wife Sītā and brother Lakṣmaṇa, you assumed the form of a sage, abducted Sītā and brought Her here.' Hanumān then informed Rāvaṇa of the pact between Sugrīva and Rāma and of how the monkey army had been deployed to search for Sītā in various places. He revealed his identity as Hanumān, one of the monkeys sent on the mission to find Sītā. He then advised Rāvaṇa, 'Get rid of your arrogance and demonic nature. It is a sin to long for the wife and wealth of another. Chant the name of Rāma. It will cleanse your impure mind. Return Sītā Dēvī and take refuge in Lord Rāma. The Lord will definitely protect one who takes refuge in Him.'

"Hearing these words, Rāvaṇa became furious. He shouted, 'Who is your Rāma? Who's Sugrīva? I shall kill both Rāma and Sītā. I shall kill you also!'

"Hanumān's response was scornful. 'Hey, evil rākṣasa! Even if a billion Rāvaṇas attack me, I will defeat them with my little finger!'

"Trembling with uncontrollable rage, Rāvaṇa commanded the rākṣasas present to kill Hanumān, but Vibhīṣaṇa, Rāvaṇa's brother, stopped the rākṣasa from attacking. He said, 'Do not kill the messenger. Doing that is not right. If you kill him, how will Rāma know what happened here? Therefore, mark him and insult him, but let him go.'

"Rāvaṇa accepted Vibhīṣaṇa's advice. He said, 'So be it. A monkey's tail is its most useful tool. He takes pride in a handsome tail. Therefore, set fire to his tail. Then parade him around the town, denouncing him as a thief.'

"The rākṣasas immediately prepared to do so."

> ***The arrogant and the foolish will not understand the advice of the wise ones. Their hearts are filled with darkness, which makes it difficult for them to distinguish right from wrong.***

39. Razing of Lanka, Return of Hanumān

Grandmother continued with the story of Rāma. "So, acting on Rāvaṇa's orders, the rākṣasas tied Hanumān's tail with a cloth dipped in oil and ghee. Hanumān sat there motionless, but his tail started growing longer and larger. Finally, all the cloth in the palace was used up. The rākṣasas went from house to house collecting cloth to tie around his tail. When that proved insufficient, they collected even costly silken robes from each house, but even then Hanumān's tail continued lengthening, demanding even more cloth to wrap around it."

Uṇṇi laughed merrily, visualizing the scene in his mind. Grandmother and Māḷu laughed along with him, enjoying young Uṇṇi's merry laughter.

"Finally the rākṣasas decided, 'Let's not spend any more time wrapping cloth around his tail. Let us set his tail on fire.'

"They set fire to the end of his tail. Hanumān slowly retracted his tail so that only the cloth was on fire. They trussed him up with a rope, and hauled him up to parade him around the town. Hanumān shrank in size, leaving behind the ropes binding him, kicked and killed his captors, and jumped up to the roof of a house. He then started leaping from roof to roof, setting fire to each house with his tail.

"Before long, Lanka was up in flames. Splendid homes were reduced to ash. Flames rose up to the skies. Lanka was being razed down. Hanumān spared the home of Vibhīṣaṇa, devotee of Śrī Rāma. The wailing of the rākṣasa women rent the air. People ran helter-skelter to save their lives. Many were burnt to a crisp. The rākṣasa women started cursing Rāvaṇa. They held him responsible for such death and destruction, which they attributed to his abducting Sītā and keeping Her captive in Lanka against Her will. Even huge trees succumbed to the flames. There was uproar everywhere.

"The Aśōka Grove, where Sītā was, was not touched by the devouring tongues of flame. After setting fire to Lanka, Hanumān extinguished the fire on his tail by dipping it into the ocean. He went to Sītā Dēvī once more, prostrated before Her, reassured Her that Śrī Rāma would save Her, and bid Her farewell. He then leapt up high to cross the ocean.

"As he did so, he let out a huge roar to let Jāmbavān and his monkey friends know of his impending arrival. They realized that Hanumān had succeeded in his mission. Within seconds, Hanumān landed on top of the Mahēndra mountains. He shouted out, loud and clear, 'I saw Her! I saw Her! By Śrī Rāmacandra's blessing, I saw Goddess Sītā!' He then came and stood before them. 'Not only that, I met Rāvaṇa and talked to him personally, and then burnt up the whole of Lanka! Come, let us go and give the news to Śrī Rāmacandra!'

"The overjoyed monkeys hugged and kissed Hanumān. All of them started together to the abode of the Lord. As they were hungry, thirsty and exhausted, they entered the Madhuvan Forest on the way there and ate fruits and honey to their hearts' content. They chased away those who came to scare them off. This was territory protected by Sugrīva. When his servants sent word to Sugrīva that a horde of monkeys was ransacking his forest, Sugrīva, instead of anger, expressed happiness at the news. He informed the Lord that Hanumān and his army of monkeys were returning after accomplishing their mission; otherwise, they would not have dared to enter Madhuvan.

"Shortly, Hanumān and the others reached Rāma and Sugrīva, and prostrated before them. Hanumān humbly recited to Śrī Rāma all the events starting from his leap across the ocean. He placed in Lord Rāma's hand the precious crest jewel that Sītā Dēvī had entrusted him. He told him the special words that Sītā had asked him to share with the Lord. Hanumān then described his meeting with Rāvaṇa, and how the meeting ended with his tail being set on fire. He narrated how he had burnt down the proud city of Lanka, after which he had bowed down once more in front of Sītā Dēvī, and then leapt back across the ocean.

"Hearing the news, Śrī Rāma was overjoyed. He said, 'O Vāyuputra! No reward from the whole world can sufficiently compensate for what you have done!' The Lord embraced Hanumān again and again, and blessed him.

"The highest duty of a human being is to worship the sacred feet of the Lord. Remembrance of the Lord destroys all misery and washes away all sin.

40. Rāma's Army Advances to Conquer Rāvaṇa

Grandma continued the narration of the *Rāmāyaṇa*. "When Rāma heard that Hanumān had seen Sītā, He was overjoyed. He congratulated Hanumān, 'O Āñjanēya,[13] you have performed a very courageous act. You have redeemed me and the solar dynasty. You not only met Sītā, you killed numerous enemies and razed Lanka. How remarkable!'

"Śrī Rāma then wondered aloud, 'How can I cross the vast ocean? How do I kill my enemies, and bring my Sītā back?'

"Hearing this, Sugrīva reassured the Lord. 'You have no cause for worry. There are monkeys with superhuman strength in our army. Together with the monkey army, we can fight Rāvaṇa and kill him. We must find a way to cross the ocean at once. I have no doubt that we will find a way soon.'

"Śrī Rāma asked Hanumān, 'Vāyuputra, kindly described the ramparts and forts of Lanka, the walls surrounding them, as well as her moats.'

"Hanumān described the city in detail. Lanka was like a gleaming golden vehicle perched on top of Trikuṭa Mountain, surrounded and defended by a wall of gold. Hanumān gave a clear and concise picture and number of the many towers, moats, bridges and defensive ramparts. He also gave Rāma the exact number of rākṣasa guards. He painted a detailed picture of the mantra hall and the

13 Son of Añjanā (Hanumān's mother).

queens' palaces. All these buildings were made of gold. Hanumān had already destroyed a quarter of Rāvaṇa's army. He said that he could cross the ocean once more and easily finish off Rāvaṇa and his rākṣasa army.

"On hearing all these details, Śrī Rāma gave orders to set out for Lanka immediately. The Lord also took into account the most auspicious time. Under Sugrīva's command, the commanders led their huge army of monkeys forward towards Lanka. Śrī Rāma and Lakṣmaṇa were in their midst, seated on the shoulders of Hanumān and Angada, the two princes radiant as the sun and the moon. The forward movement of the army resembled the advancing waves of the mighty ocean. They approached the ocean's northern shore by the flanks of the Mahēndra mountains. By the time they reached the beach, the sun had set. They performed their evening prayers, and then began working out a plan to cross the ocean. The monkeys were alarmed, wondering how they were going to cross the vast expanse of water."

Uṇṇi was listening with great enthusiasm. Patting her eager grandson, Grandma continued, "Now, let us see what Rāvaṇa was up to in Lanka."

Uṇṇi asked, "Did Rāvaṇa know that Lord Rāma and his army of monkeys were advancing towards Lanka?"

Grandmother said, "Of course, Uṇṇi. Rāvaṇa had many spies. He called his council of ministers and said, 'Our enemies have reached the sea shore. From Hanumān's exploits, we know that they are brave and strong. Therefore, they will somehow find a way to cross the ocean and enter Lanka. How can we resist, thwart and defeat them? Formulate a plan and let me know.'

"The ministers reassured Rāvaṇa. One of them said, 'You have conquered all the three worlds. Your son Mēghanād bound Indra up and brought him here. You defeated Vaiśravaṇa and confiscated the puṣpaka-vimāna. Even the Lord of Death fears you. All your enemies have surrendered to your might. This Śrī Rāma is only a worm, a worm in human form. The only reason that the monkey could cause so much damage was that we were negligent in our counter-attack. None of us anticipated his moves. If we had known, that monkey would not have escaped alive. Now, we need not fear those monkeys or men. Lord, command one of us. We shall take it upon ourselves to kill all of them!'

"Thus, the foolish ministers allayed the doubts of Rāvaṇa, who became overconfident."

> ***There will be many people to speak words we like. Many will make us feel great and good. The foolish will fall for their words. Owing to arrogance and ignorance, they will not heed sound advice.***

41. Brotherly Advice

Grandmother continued with the story of the valiant Prince Rāma.

"On hearing the encouraging words of his ministers, Rāvaṇa felt relieved and began to relax. It was then that a herald announced the arrival of Kumbhakarṇa. Rāvaṇa was happy that his strong brother had awoken from sleep and arrived to meet him at the moment when he was most needed."

"Grandma, who is Kumbhakarṇa?" asked Uṇṇi. "Is he a rākṣasa?"

"Kumbhakarṇa was Rāvaṇa's younger brother. Do you know what was unique about him? He would sleep continuously for six months. He would then wake up and be fresh for a day, after which he would go back to sleep for another six months."

"My God!" said Uṇṇi, "What a sleepyhead! When did he eat?" Uṇṇi asked in amazement.

"When he woke up, he would eat six months' worth of food in one day. You can imagine what a grand feast it would be!"

Uṇṇi laughed, picturing the idea of Kumbhakarṇa waking up for only one day in six months.

Grandma continued, "Anyway, Kumbhakarṇa had woken up and come to greet his brother. It is difficult to describe his sheer size and strength. His very appearance frightened people, though Rāvaṇa was relieved to see his fearsome younger brother. He embraced Kumbhakarṇa and offered him a seat. Then he recounted all the events that had happened until then. Listening to his tale, Kumbhakarṇa said in great fear, 'Elder brother, did you perpetrate this grave injustice, considering Rāma to be an ordinary person? Rāma is no mere mortal, but the very incarnation of Lord Viṣṇu. If you value your life, take refuge in Rāma. You have done great wrong. If you do not like what I say, I am ready to go and kill Rāma and His army.'

"Rāvaṇa's son, Indrajit, was standing near him, listening to the conversation. He said, 'Father, I shall go to war. Please permit me to do so. I shall kill Rāma and the army of monkeys, and return at once!'

"It was at this moment that another brother of Rāvaṇa, Vibhīṣaṇa, came to meet him. Rāvaṇa embraced him with great affection and seated his brother next to him. Vibhīṣaṇa was an ardent devotee of Śrī Rāma, and he wanted to persuade his elder brother to mend his ways. He said, 'Elder brother, please listen patiently to what I am going to say. There is no one in this world strong enough to defeat Rāmacandra. Your aggression will destroy our race. Neither Kumbhakarṇa nor Indrajit can win a battle with Rāma. He is the incarnation of Lord Nārāyaṇa. Therefore, take Sītā Dēvī at once to Lord Rāma and take refuge in Him. Beg for His grace. Rāma is very compassionate. He will never forsake anyone who seeks refuge in Him. He will forgive all your faults and grant you refuge. Do not be taken in by the words of your empty-headed ministers. They will not be there to support you in distress. Return Sītā Dēvī to Lord Rāma and rule Lanka wisely. Do not cause the ruin of your race!'

"Vibhīṣaṇa went on to recount the many instances in which Rāma had acted to uphold dharma. Rāvaṇa could no longer control his anger. He said, "Vibhīṣaṇa, stop! You are my enemy, not my relative. Do not speak such words to me anymore. I shall not consider you my brother. I shall kill you!'

"Hearing this threat, Vibhīṣaṇa thought, 'I have tried my best to talk sense into my cruel brother. I realize that no one can change the fate decreed by God. My only refuge is the feet of Lord Rāma. I shall spend the rest of my life under His protective shelter.' He decided to renounce all his wealth and power, and to leave Lanka. He stood with joined palms and bowed down before his elder brother. He wanted to say goodbye.

"Rāvaṇa understood his younger brother's thoughts. Boiling with rage, he said, 'Go! Go and serve your Rāma! If you do not leave Lanka now, you shall be at the receiving end of my candrahāsa!'

"Vibhīṣaṇa replied, 'You are equal to my father, and so, I shall obey your command. I shall leave you now to take refuge in Śrī Rāma.'

"Vibhīṣaṇa tried once more to warn his brother about the impending danger, but his words fell on deaf ears. Bidding farewell to Rāvaṇa, Vibhīṣaṇa left the palace."

> ***God's will always prevails. But if we take refuge in the Lord, He will save us.***

42. Vibhīṣaṇa in Śrī Rāma's Presence

Grandmother, Māḷu and Uṇṇi entered the pūjā room. They garlanded the picture of Śrī Rāmacandra and lit the oil lamp. Grandma closed her eyes and prayed to Lord Rāma. Then, she asked Uṇṇi, "Where did we stop yesterday?"

Uṇṇi said, "Vibhīṣaṇa was leaving Lanka to seek refuge in Śrī Rāma, and to join Him in the war against adharma."

Grandmother said, "Oh yes. Vibhīṣaṇa travelled through the air with four other ministers, crossed the ocean, and came to a stop in mid-air, right above where Śrī Rāma, Lord of all beings, was seated. By His mere presence, Rāma was blessing the monkey army. In humble tones loud enough for them all to hear, Vibhīṣaṇa said, 'Śrī Rāmacandra, victory to You! I am Vibhīṣaṇa, brother of Rāvaṇa. I am Your devotee, and am here to serve You. I tried hard to knock some sense into my brother. I advised him and warned him, but my cruel brother did not heed my words. On the contrary, he was ready to kill me with his candrahāsa. I consider Your feet my refuge. I have abandoned Lanka to take refuge in You. Please grant me refuge!'

"Hearing Vibhīṣaṇa's request, a doubt arose in Sugrīva's mind. He said, 'O Lord Rāma! The rākṣasas cannot be trusted. Vibhīṣaṇa is a rākṣasa and Rāvaṇa's brother. He is well armed. The ministers accompanying him might well be conjurers up to no good. Who knows, they might have come here to kill us! Therefore, allow me to kill them.'

"Hearing this, Hanumān said, 'Lord, from what I know, Vibhīṣaṇa is an ideal devotee. He came here believing in You. Not only that, there is good and bad in every race and clan. In my humble opinion, You must grant Vibhīṣaṇa refuge.'

"Having heard both opinions, the Lord said, 'I shall accept Hanumān's opinion in this matter. It is the duty of a king to protect those who seek refuge in him, whoever he or she may be. It is sinful to abandon those who seek refuge, but meritorious to save them and protect them from all harm. Therefore, bring Vibhīṣaṇa to me!'

"Vibhīṣaṇa came in front of the Lord and sang hymns in praise of Lord Rāma. "Śrī Rāmacandra, treasure-trove of compassion, prostrations to You. Bless me and save me. You are mother, father and creator of the whole universe and all its beings. I long to attain You through true devotion. O Rāmacandra, I bow down before You again and again!' Vibhīṣaṇa spoke about universal principles and the Supreme Self.

"Pleased with Vibhīṣaṇa's knowledge and devotion, Śrī Rāma said, 'Ask what you want from me. If you see me once, then you shall never again know sorrow!'

"Vibhīṣaṇa wanted only unceasing devotion to Śrī Rāma. With joy, the Lord said, 'Meditate constantly on me. You shall attain Liberation. Those who sing the hymn you sang in my praise will also attain Liberation, if they sing it with great devotion.

"Summoning Lakṣmaṇa, Rāma asked him to bring some water from the ocean. With great fanfare, the Lord anointed Vibhīṣaṇa King of Lanka. The dēvas were thrilled. Sugrīva hugged Vibhīṣaṇa warmly and requested his help in killing their enemy, Rāvaṇa. Smiling, Vibhīṣaṇa replied, 'Why would Rāma, Lord of the universe, need our help in anything? We are only serving Him, not helping Him!' Hearing this, Sugrīva was relieved and happy.

"In the meantime, Rāvaṇa sent a rākṣasa messenger named Śuka to Rāma. The messenger hovered in the air and conveyed a message from Rāvaṇa to Sugrīva: 'Your brother Vālī is my closest relative. Why should you, younger brother of the great Vālī, be loyal to Rāma? There is no need for Sugrīva to become angry with me just because I abducted Sītā Dēvī. In fact, it is none of his business. Therefore, if he wants to maintain his stature, it is better for him to give up his friendship with Śrī Rāma and to return to his kingdom. This is what Rāvaṇa commands!'

"Hearing these words, the monkeys leapt up high and started pummelling Śuka with their hard fists. Unable to bear the pain, he cried out to Śrī Rāma for help. 'O Śrī Rāma, ocean of compassion, have mercy on me! Do not kill the messenger. Please act with justice. Save me from these monkeys!'

"When He heard this, Śrī Rāma ordered the monkeys to stop attacking Śuka. Nevertheless, He told them not to send Śuka back immediately, but to imprison him. The monkeys tied Śuka up. Another rākṣasa named Śārdūla, also sent by Rāvaṇa, was hovering in the air and watching all these events. Frightened, he flew back to Rāvaṇa and told him what had happened. Fear crept into Rāvaṇa's mind. Pondering how to save himself, he sighed deeply."

> ***There will be good and bad people of all races, castes and colours.***

43. Building of the Bridge, Dialogue between Rāvaṇa and Śuka

Grandmother continued with the narration of the *Rāmāyaṇa*, the adventures of the brave and compassionate Prince Rāma.

"Thus the monkeys captured Śuka and imprisoned him. Śrī Rāma then said to Vibhīṣaṇa, Sugrīva and the others, 'Let us think of a way to cross the ocean.'

"All of them discussed matters and decided to first please Varuṇa, God of the Ocean. Śrī Rāma spread the holy darbha grass on the seashore and prostrated to Varuṇa with humility and devotion. But even after Śrī Rāma had continuously worshipped the ocean for three days and nights, the sea waves did not subside and Varuṇa did not appear. Śrī Rāma became extremely angry. Śrī Rāmacandra has complete control over his emotions, Uṇṇi. He is calm and peaceful at all times. But when He became enraged with the ocean, He commanded Lakṣmaṇa to bring Him His bow and arrows. Rāma said, 'How dare Varuṇa show such arrogance? My ancestors increased the size of the oceans. For the arrogance he has shown me, I am going to dry up the ocean! Let the monkeys cross the ocean by foot.'

"Seeing Lord Rāma's wrath, all the beings in the world began to tremble in fear. Varuṇa, frightened by the Lord's threat, surfaced with priceless gems which he placed humbly before Rāma. Then, prostrating before Him, Varuṇa said, 'Save me! You created me as water. I cannot help being true to my fluid nature. Please do not dry me up. Protect me, I take refuge in You. I shall show You the easiest path to Lanka.'

"The Lord's anger abated, but the arrow He had been about to release could not remain unused. So, on Varuṇa's advice, the Lord released the arrow towards Drumakulya in the north, where cruel rākṣasas lived. The arrow sped away, killed them all, came back and settled into Rāma's quiver.

"Varuṇa bowed down humbly and said, 'Lord, the monkey named Nala is the son of Viśvakarma, and thus most qualified for this task. Let him build a bridge to Lanka. Everyone can then walk to Lanka.

"Nala immediately came up and bowed before the Lord. He instructed the monkey army to uproot mountains and huge rocks and trees. Nala then started building a dam to contain the waters. Śrī Rāma installed an idol of Lord Śiva on the spot where the bridge was to start. Everyone prostrated before the idol of Lord Śiva. This spot has since become a place of pilgrimage, and is known today as Rāmēśvaram."

Uṇṇi asked, "Did the monkeys finish building the bridge, Grandma?"

"Of course, their hearts were brimming with love for Śrī Rāma. Each monkey worked hard under the supervision of Nala, and the bridge was completed in five days. The monkeys started walking fearlessly on the bridge that spanned the ocean.

"Śrī Rāma travelled on the strong shoulders of Hanumān. Lakṣmaṇa travelled on Angada's broad shoulders. When they reached Lanka, they climbed up Mount Subēla. The city of Lanka was stretched out below them. Just as Hanumān had described, Lanka was glittering like gold. Śrī Rāma took in every small detail: the flag posts, forts, banners, palaces and towers, among other things. He saw Rāvaṇa sitting inside his palatial chambers, surrounded by royal finery and his ministers. Laughing, Lord Rāma said, 'Hey, monkeys, release Śuka. Let him go and inform Rāvaṇa of our arrival, and about how we walked to Lanka after building a bridge across the ocean.'

"The monkeys freed Śuka, who scurried to Rāvaṇa and bowed down before him. Rāvaṇa asked him, 'Why did you delay in returning? You look tired. Did the monkeys harm you?'

"With great humility, Śuka said, 'O Lord of Lanka, let me share with you words that are in your best interests. Please hear me out. I travelled through the air and arrived where Sugrīva was sitting. I hovered in mid-air and told Sugrīva all that you had instructed me to say. The monkeys caught hold of me and started punching me. When I saw that they were going to kill me, I cried out to Śrī Rāma to save me. Rāma is compassionate. He ordered the monkeys to release me, a mere messenger. He also ordered that I should be held captive for the time being. The monkeys built a bridge across the ocean and are now in Lanka. Vibhīṣaṇa, your brother, is also with them. After releasing me, Rāma told me to convey a message to you. Please listen: "Release Sītā, or else, prepare for war. I shall totally annihilate you and your army!"'

"Śuka then showed Rāvaṇa the monkey army on top of Mount Subēla and described the might of the likes of Nala, Angada, Jāmbavān and Hanumān. He also spoke about how transient life on earth was. Śuka told Rāvaṇa that it was impossible to win a war against Rāma. He advised Rāvaṇa to give up his arrogance and to surrender to Rāma.

"Though Śuka's advice was wise and meant to dispel ignorance, Rāvaṇa could not appreciate it. Outraged, he roared, 'You are my servant, and you dare advise me? I am letting you off the hook now in return for a service you did me long ago. Get out! Or I shall finish you off in a minute!'

"In great fear, Śuka left for his home at once."

> ***There is a seed of devotion within each one of us. It will germinate only when the climate is right. The moment we experience God's divine power, the seed of devotion will germinate and grow into a mighty tree.***

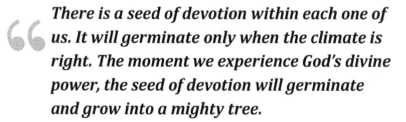

44. Story of Śuka, Words of Mālyavān

Uṇṇi asked, "Grandma, why didn't Rāvaṇa kill Śuka?"

Grandma replied, "Śuka was his trusted servant. Rāvaṇa remembered the many services Śuka had faithfully rendered, and so let him go. The minute he was let off, Śuka returned to his former home.

"Uṇṇi, I would like you to know the story of Śuka, before he became Rāvaṇa's servant. He was not really a rākṣasa but a good Brāhmin. He lived in the forest with his wife, performing many yajñas for the prosperity of the dēvas and the destruction of the rākṣasas. In those days, there was a rākṣasa named Vajradramṣṭra, who was an important leader of the demons. He was looking for an opportunity to harm Śuka.

"One day, Sage Agastya visited the hermitage of Śuka, who invited him to stay for lunch. When Agastya went to take a bath, the wicked Vajradramṣṭra assumed the form of Agastya and came to Śuka and asked him to cook meat for his lunch. Śuka asked his wife to prepare meat dishes. Later, when the real Agastya sat down for lunch, Vajradramṣṭra took on the form of Śuka's wife and served human meat to Agastya and then disappeared. Seeing human flesh on his leaf, Sage Agastya cursed Śuka, 'O cruel Brāhmin! You tried to feed me the flesh of a human being. I curse you to become a man-eating rākṣasa!'

"When he heard Sage Agastya's curse, Śuka became agitated. He said, 'O great sage! It was you who had ordered me to serve you meat! Why do you curse me now?'

"The sage intuitively realized what had happened. Feeling remorseful, he said, 'O Brāhmin, you are innocent! It was the rākṣasa who tricked us. Even I did not understand the real situation. But my curse always works. Therefore, let me give you an auspicious means by which the curse can be lifted. Rāvaṇa will abduct Śrī Rāma's wife and keep her captive in his garden at Lanka. You will be in Lanka, serving Rāvaṇa with utmost sincerity. When Rāmacandra comes prepared for war, Rāvaṇa will send you as his messenger to Rāma. You will come back to Rāvaṇa, and advise him on the nature of the Self, on truth and honour, and the path to God. The curse will be lifted from you and you will regain your former form.'

"Thus, the curse was lifted from Śuka and he went back to his home in the forest.

"It was then that Mālyavān, Rāvaṇa's maternal grandfather, came to the court to meet Rāvaṇa. Mālyavān was wise and intelligent. He tried to counsel Rāvaṇa: 'Śrī Rāma is not an ordinary human being. He is Lord Nārāyaṇa himself. Take Sītā back to Her Lord. Prostrate at His feet. Ever since you stole Sītā and brought her here, Lanka has seen many omens foretelling doom. You must not be the cause of our destruction. Even though you have a cruel mind, if you sincerely worship Lord Rāma, your mind will become clean and pure. Obey my words!'

"Rāvaṇa was not at all willing to listen to Mālyavān's words. He said, "Grandpa, why do you praise Rāma so highly? Why do you fear Him? He is a fool who thinks that He can defeat me with an army of monkeys. Do not repeat these words of yours or try to advise me on this matter. I don't like it! Please go back home!'

"Accompanied by his ministers, Rāvaṇa climbed up to the top of his palace and looked out. Sitting there, he saw the army of monkeys on one side of Rāma. He realized that they were formidable opponents, both in size and strength. From afar, Śrī Rāma could also see Rāvaṇa, standing like a mountain, with crowns glittering on his 10 heads."

"*Those who are full of pride will drown in the sea of ignorance. It is very difficult to guide them towards the light of knowledge.*

45. War Begins

Uṇṇi and Māḷu prostrated before the picture of Śrī Rāma before sitting down to hear Grandma continue the narration.

Uṇṇi asked curiously, "Did the war start, Grandma?"

Grandma said, "Rāma saw Rāvaṇa surveying his army, his expression devoid of the least bit of regret. Enraged, Rāma took an arrow from Lakṣmaṇa, aimed it, and let it fly. A split second later, the ten crowns of Rāvaṇa and his ceremonial parasol crashed to the ground. Rāvaṇa was mortified. He rushed down and commanded his army chiefs, 'Let the war begin! It is not manly to hide indoors.'

"The rākṣasas, armed with various weapons, got into different kinds of vehicles at once, and set out to the battlefield to the sound of beating drums and blaring trumpets. The commanders divided the forces and stationed the divisions at the four entrances to the towers. Śrī Rāma's army also divided itself into four groups, and stationed themselves in the four directions. The monkeys started lifting rocks and mountains, and uprooting trees. They aimed well and hurled the huge boulders and trees, destroying many parts of Lanka. They pulverized the strong, high fort walls and filled up the deep moats.

"The rākṣasas started firing all kinds of weapons at the monkey army. Many soldiers died on either side. Rāvaṇa sent rākṣasas over to spy on Śrī Rāma's army. These rākṣasas disguised themselves as monkeys and penetrated the enemy camp, but the real monkeys found them out. You can imagine what happened next. They started beating up the rākṣasas disguised as monkeys. When the rākṣasas started screaming in pain, Lord Rāma, who was compassionate, ordered the monkeys to stop hitting them and set them free.

"Meanwhile, many were telling Rāvaṇa that it was impossible to defeat Śrī Rāma. Using black magic, the evil king conjured up the head and bow of Rāma and laid it in front of Sītā, proclaiming that he had killed her Lord. Sītā swooned in grief. After Rāvaṇa left, Vibhīṣaṇa's wife consoled Sītā and convinced her that it was just an illusion Rāvaṇa had conjured.

"An infernal war raged between the two armies. Angada killed all the rākṣasas who challenged him. The sound and fury of the war began to vibrate throughout the world. The sounds of elephants and horses, the movements of the chariot wheels, the hoarse cries of the rākṣasas, and the chatter of the monkeys created a dreadful cacophony. Even the dēvas watched the fight from the heavens above.

"When Indrajit, the son of Rāvaṇa, came face to face with Angada, the latter killed Indrajit's charioteer.

Sugrīva, Hanumān and Vibhīṣaṇa fought and killed powerful rākṣasas. Indrajit had a powerful weapon with him, the *Nāgāstra*, the snake arrow. He used the Nāgāstra to great effect, causing the monkey army and even Rāma and Lakṣmaṇa to faint and collapse. There was great sorrow in the world. Indrajit blew the victory horn as he returned to the palace."

Uṇṇi looked sad and gloomy. He said, "Grandma, how horrible! Even Lord Rāma has fallen! What will happen now?"

Grandma continued, "Listen, Uṇṇi. There was a rush of mighty wings that shook the whole world. The light of a million suns spread all around."

Uṇṇi asked anxiously, "Who was it, Grandma?"

"Uṇṇi, it was Garuḍa himself, who had come down from Vaikuṇṭha. Garuḍa landed at Lord Rāma's feet and bowed down before Him. As snakes are powerless before eagles, with Garuḍa's arrival, the snakes that had bound the monkey army, Rāma and Lakṣmaṇa became helpless and powerless. The army regained its spirits and started fighting with renewed vigour. Rāvaṇa realized that all the monkeys who had been killed by Indrajit had come back to life. He summoned the rākṣasa named

Dhūmrakṣa and said, 'Dhūmrakṣa, kill all those arrogant monkeys and come back to me.'

"A fierce fight erupted between Hanumān and Dhūmrakṣa. Finally, Hanumān killed him. Numerous monkeys and rākṣasas died on the battlefield. The war continued. The monkeys fought with stones, boulders, mountains and trees, and the rākṣasas, with their weapons.

"Rāvaṇa then picked the strongest rākṣasas and sent them to battle, but each and every one of them was killed by Rāma's army."

“ ***It is wrong to use sorcery or black magic to defeat an enemy. One might succeed in the beginning but such tricks invariably end in disaster.***

46. Rāvaṇa's Preparations

Grandmother continued with the *Rāmāyaṇa*. "The commander in chief of Rāvaṇa's army was Prahasta, a very strong rākṣasa. He, along with four ministers and the army of rākṣasas, faced the monkey army. Rivers of blood overran the ground. Finally, Jāmbavān, a simian of immense strength, killed all four ministers. Nīla killed Prahasta. When he heard this, Rāvaṇa arrogantly said, 'I am going to the battlefield. Prepare the royal chariot. Let the army follow me.'

"Rāvaṇa and his elite force started preparations for the war. Rāma saw Rāvaṇa and his warriors from afar. Smiling at Vibhīṣaṇa, He said, 'Please give me all the details of the rākṣasas advancing to the battlefront.'

"Vibhīṣaṇa described the strong points of each rākṣasa in great detail. 'The fat rākṣasa is Atikāya. He is one of the sons of Rāvaṇa. Standing near him is Indrajit, another one of his sons. Sitting on top of the elephant is Mahōdara. The one holding the iron pestle in his hand is Narāntaka. On the far side are Kumbha and Nikumbha, the sons of Kumbhakarṇa.'

"When Rāvaṇa saw that all his sons were accompanying him to the battlefront, he said, 'Go back and defend the palace. I can fight this army all by myself!'"

Uṇṇi was listening intently to the story. He looked as if he was in the battlefield along with Rāma and Rāvaṇa. Grandmother continued, "Rāvaṇa split the monkey army with his weapons. Lord Rāma prepared for war.

Lakṣmaṇa requested him, 'Let me fight him first.' The Lord agreed to His brother's earnest plea.

"Hanumān could not contain his anger when he saw Rāvaṇa, abductor of Sītā Dēvī. He said, 'I am the one who killed your son, Akṣay Kumār. I shall do the same to you.'

"In a split second, Hanumān pounced on Rāvaṇa and whacked him with his pestle. Rāvaṇa shuddered as he fell to the ground under the force of the blow. He thought, 'This is a mighty beast!' and said to Hanumān, 'You are by no means an insignificant monkey.'

"Hanumān replied, 'None have survived my blows but you are still alive. This means that I have lost my strength. Nevertheless, let us engage in battle.'

"Before Hanumān had finished speaking, Rāvaṇa struck him hard and Hanumān fell unconscious. Seeing this, Nīla jumped atop Rāvaṇa's head's and started dancing, stamping on his ten heads and their crowns. Rāvaṇa used the *Āgnēyāstra,*[14] and Nīla was flung afar. He also fell to the ground.

"Lakṣmaṇa came forward swiftly and started showering arrows at the powerful Rāvaṇa. They rained so fast that no one could even see the battle ground. Lakṣmaṇa then knocked Rāvaṇa's bow to the ground. The rākṣasa king grabbed the spear that Maya had given him and hurled it at Lakṣmaṇa's chest. Lakṣmaṇa fell unconscious when the spear hit his chest. Rāvaṇa ran

14 Weapon emitting inextinguishable flames.

to where he lay and tried to lift Lakṣmaṇa, but failed to nudge him even an inch. Rāvaṇa was celebrated for his formidable strength. He had once lifted the Kailāsa Mountain and played with it. Now, finding himself unable to lift Lakṣmaṇa, Rāvaṇa realized that it was Śrī Rāma's will power that was preventing him from even moving Lakṣmaṇa's body a bit. He felt ashamed.

"Hanumān, who had recovered from the blow, ran to Lakṣmaṇa, picked him up as if he were a flower, laid him down at Rāma's feet, and bowed down before the Lord. Maya's spear, hitherto adhering to Lakṣmaṇa's chest, moved back to Rāvaṇa. Rāma, incandescent with rage, started fighting with Rāvaṇa. He said, 'Hey rākṣasa! I have finally come face to face with you. I shall kill you and all the rākṣasas with you!'

"A fierce battle ensued. Some of Rāvaṇa's arrows pierced Hanumān's body. Seeing this, a furious Rāma released an arrow aimed at Rāvaṇa's chest. Rāvaṇa fell unconscious to the ground. Rāma then destroyed his chariot, ceremonial parasol and crown. The Lord, who was just even in warfare, would not kill an enemy who was defenceless and weaponless. He said, 'Hey rākṣasa! I see that you are defenceless. Go back to Lanka. Come back tomorrow, ready to fight!' A shamed Rāvaṇa retreated to his palace, where he sat on his throne, lost in thought.

"The Lord treated Lakṣmaṇa and the wounded monkeys with *Siddha* medicine,[15] and they recovered completely.

"As he sat despondently on the throne, Rāvaṇa said to those standing near him, 'I think good times have ended for Lanka. All the merit I gained from previous lives have been exhausted. I have earned the curses of many great souls as well as chaste and devoted wives. Are those curses coming into effect now? Wake Kumbhakarṇa up from his sleep. My strong brother will be able to defeat Śrī Rāma.'

"The rākṣasas strove hard to wake up the slumbering giant."

> ***The rules of war forbid the use of weapons against weak opponents who are unable to fight back.***

15 Traditional medicine of South India.

47. Kumbhakarṇa's Plea for Peace, Kumbhakarṇa's Death

Grandmother continued, "The rākṣasas tried hard to wake up Kumbhakarṇa, who was as big and strong as a mountain. A division of the army clambered onto his chest and ran to and fro. They poured pots of water into his ears. But he did not even stir. His snores became louder. Then, with the help of elephants, the rākṣasas tried to pluck the hair from Kumbhakarṇa's nostrils. Even then, Kumbhakarṇa did not stir. Instead, the hairs inside his nostrils lacerated the trunks of the elephants! The rākṣasas pounded on huge drums, blared trumpets, and clanked cymbals near his ear."

Uṇṇi laughed and laughed. He rolled around laughing and finally fell into Māḷu's lap. Grandma chuckled and continued.

"After a long time, aroused by all the din, Kumbhakarṇa stretched his huge body and started to rise. The rākṣasas, fearing for their lives, ran and hid from his sight. He blinked and slowly opened his eyes. Kumbhakarṇa always started feasting the moment he opened his eyes. The rākṣasas had prepared pots filled with blood and alcohol, mounds of rice and curry, and other dishes he liked. Kumbhakarṇa devoured all the food in a trice, and his belly became bloated. He then asked why he had been woken up unusually early. The rākṣasas explained to him all that had been taking place in the battlefield. Kumbhakarṇa said, 'If that's the case, I shall get my elder brother's blessings and immediately go to the battlefield.'

"Kumbhakarṇa walked to Rāvaṇa's palace. Rāvaṇa was very pleased to see his younger brother. All his hopes for victory now rested on Kumbhakarṇa. Hugging Kumbhakarṇa tightly, Rāvaṇa gave him a detailed description of all that had transpired so far. Rāvaṇa said, 'Rāma has come to war, accompanied by an army of monkeys, but they are not to be taken lightly. They have killed capable and strong warriors like Prahasta. When I fought with Rāma, I was almost killed by Him. You are my only hope now. Kill Rāma, Lakṣmaṇa and the army of monkeys!'

"Rāvaṇa's request took Kumbhakarṇa by surprise. He said, 'I see that my elder brother is not able to discriminate between right and wrong. In that case, you must listen to people who know the difference between the two. I had told you to return Sītā to Rāma. Vibhīṣaṇa said the same thing. But in your anger, you banished him from the kingdom. In times of danger, some people lose their good sense. Even if people tell them the right course of action, the foolish will not heed good advice. Your desire for Sītā will lead to the destruction of our race. Sītā and Rāma are incarnations of God. Do not think that you can kill them. It is better for you to seek refuge in Rāma and to live in peace and prosperity.'

"Rāvaṇa burst out in anger, 'Younger brother, I did not wake you up with great difficulty to hear you preach! I woke you up to fight with Rāma. Go and fight, if you can. Otherwise, go back to sleep!'

"Hearing this, Kumbhakarṇa lifted his heavy spear and walked into the battlefield. He thought, 'It is better to die at the hands of Śrī Rāmacandra and attain eternal liberation than to live under the rule of my cruel elder brother!'

"When the monkeys saw Kumbhakarṇa advancing upon them like a huge mountain, they ran away and hid themselves in fear. Kumbhakarṇa was so tall that he could reach up and touch the skies. Śrī Rāma asked Vibhīṣaṇa who he was, and the latter replied, 'It is Kumbhakarṇa, my elder brother and Rāvaṇa's younger brother. It is impossible to win a battle with him.'

"Vibhīṣaṇa ran swiftly to his elder brother and said, 'Elder brother, I bow down before you. I tried very hard to convince our brother to return Sītā to Rāma and to seek refuge in Him but he did not listen. On the contrary, he unsheathed his sword and threatened to kill me. I then came to Śrī Rāmacandra and sought refuge in him.'

"Even though Kumbhakarṇa was a fearsome rākṣasa, he was just and did not appreciate Rāvaṇa's evil intentions. He discriminated between good and bad. Hugging his younger brother with great affection, Kumbhakarṇa said, 'You are indeed blessed. Save the future of our race by serving Rāma. But I have decided to fight the war on behalf of our brother out of love and a sense of duty towards him.'

"Vibhīṣaṇa bowed down before Kumbhakarṇa and returned to Śrī Rāma.

"Kumbhakarṇa made preparations for war, and soon became angry enough to fight hard. He started killing the monkeys with his hands and feet. Fearing for their lives, the monkeys scattered in all directions. In a trice, Kumbhakarṇa killed many monkeys. Sugrīva uprooted a huge mountain and hurled it at the giant rākṣasa, but it did not make a dent. It bounced off his chest and fell down. Kumbhakarṇa then threw his spear at Sugrīva, and it landed on his chest, knocking Sugrīva unconscious. Kumbhakarṇa carried the unconscious Sugrīva away, as if he had already won the war.

"Seeing this, the rākṣasa women rejoiced. From the balconies of their homes, they sprinkled jasmine essence and threw garlands dipped in sandal essence at Kumbhakarṇa. When the cool drops of jasmine and sandal and the garlands touched Sugrīva, he regained consciousness. He bit off Kumbhakarṇa's nose and ears and leapt into the skies. Feeling humiliated, Kumbhakarṇa ran back to the battlefield, as blood streamed down his face. Lakṣmaṇa shot several arrows at him. Kumbhakarṇa grabbed monkeys and started gobbling them up. Then he turned against Lord Rāmacandra, who lopped off Kumbhakarṇa's right hand, which held the spear. Rāma then cut off his left hand and both legs. Finally, Rāma used the *Indrāstra* to behead Kumbhakarṇa. His body fell into the ocean, and the severed head, at the gates of the tower. Thus the terrible Kumbhakarṇa was killed. The gods in heaven showered flowers on Rāma and praised Him for ridding the world of this terrible menace.

"Sage Nārada came down to earth and praised Lord Rāma with great devotion. Nārada prophesied that Lakṣmaṇa would kill Indrajit and that Rāma would kill Rāvaṇa. Nārada then vanished."

" ***Owing to their companionship with the ignorant, many people oppose divine beings even when they are aware of their divinity. Such people will eventually be defeated. Kumbhakarṇa is a good example.***

48. Atikāya's Death, Indrajit's Victory

Grandmother continued with the *Rāmāyaṇa*. "When Rāvaṇa heard about the death of his brother, he was so shocked that he fell unconscious. When he regained his senses, he started lamenting Kumbhakarṇa's death. Eight leading rākṣasa warriors approached Rāvaṇa: Triśiras, Atikāya, Dēvāntaka, Narāntaka, Mahōdara, Mahāpārśva, Mattan and Unmattan. They told Rāvaṇa, 'We shall go into the battlefield and kill Rāma!'

"When he heard this, Rāvaṇa was consoled and slightly relieved, and told them to go ahead. When the monkeys saw the eight rākṣasas approaching, they started hurling stones, mountains and trees at the rākṣasas, who started fighting back. The two sides were well-matched. A river of blood started to flow. The rākṣasas suffered most. Angada killed Narāntaka. Hanumān, Angada, Nīla and Ṛṣabha together killed six of the other remaining rākṣasas. Only Atikāya remained alive. A skilled archer, he rode proudly into the battlefield on a chariot drawn by a thousand horses. The monkeys ran off in great fear. Seeing this, Lakṣmaṇa went to fight with Atikāya. However, all his arrows were not able to make a dent in Atikāya's armour. Vāyu, God of the Winds, appeared before Lakṣmaṇa in human form, and said, 'Atikāya is wearing body armour that Lord Brahmā gifted him. Spears cannot harm him. Use the Brahmāstra on him.'

"Lakṣmaṇa meditated upon Śrī Rāma, and then hurled the Brahmāstra, which severed Atikāya's head.

The monkeys carried the head and placed it at Śrī Rāma's feet. With palms joined in devotion, the monkeys bowed down before Him.

"The remaining rākṣasas, enfeebled and reduced in number, went back to Rāvaṇa and told him about the defeat and death of his eight powerful rākṣasa warriors. Rāvaṇa shook in fear. In great anguish, he roared, 'What shall I do now? My ministers and army commanders have all been killed. I have become helpless!'

"Indrajit, who had just entered and heard his father's lament, came before his father and prostrated. He said, 'Why grieve when I am alive? Trust me: the end of our enemies is near. Bless me and allow me to enter the fray.'

"Indrajit's words gave some consolation to Rāvaṇa, who said, 'Win the war, and come back to me.'

"Indrajit performed a sacred fire sacrifice to Lord Śiva in order to increase his prowess in war. His fire sacrifice was performed in a hidden cave named Nikumbhila. With the blessings of Agni, the God of Fire, Indrajit gained mastery over and possession of many weapons as well as the ability to appear and disappear at will. He stepped into the battlefield. The monkeys faced him with vigour. The fight started.

"Indrajit's arrows fell like rain on the army of monkeys, who fought back valiantly. The battle intensified. When he saw the large numbers of rākṣasas dying on the battlefield, Indrajit became upset and angry. He disappeared, hid himself in the skies, and used the Brahmāstra on the army of monkeys. The monkeys started falling down unconscious. A hundred arrows struck Sugrīva, who also fell unconscious. This conjurer single-handedly defeated many million monkeys! Rāma and Lakṣmaṇa were astonished as they could not see anybody around. Before they realized what was happening, Indrajit struck Rāma and Lakṣmaṇa with his arrows, knocking them down. When he saw this, Indrajit took out his conch and arrogantly sounded the victory note, before returning to the palace.

"The sages and dēvas were confounded and deeply worried, as Śrī Rāma and Lakṣmaṇa were leaders of the battle. They and commanders like Sugrīva were all lying motionless on the ground. Who could rouse Rāma and Lakṣmaṇa? Only Vibhīṣaṇa, Rāvaṇa's brother. He was standing afar, watching everything."

> **_Good and evil are equally strong. Only by God's grace can one conquer evil. Even an incarnation of God had to reel under the blows of evil for a short spell._**

49. Hanumān's Quest for the Elixir, Kālanēmi's Tactics

Uṇṇi said, "Grandma, that's terrible. Śrī Rāma, Lakṣmaṇa and all the monkeys are unconscious. Who will fight now? Who will defeat Rāvaṇa?"

Grandma said, "I'll tell you, Uṇṇi. Didn't I say that someone was watching the battle from afar? Someone who saw that Rāma, Lakṣmaṇa and all the monkeys had fallen? They were unconscious because they could not fight against an Indrajit who had disappeared into the skies. Who was it, Uṇṇi? Do you remember?"

Uṇṇi said, "Vibhīṣaṇa."

Grandma said, "Yes, Vibhīṣaṇa indeed. He had stayed hidden on purpose. Indrajit had returned to the palace. When dusk fell, Vibhīṣaṇa lit a flaming torch and walked amongst the fallen, checking to see which ones were alive. Hanumān was also walking around the battlefield all by himself, checking to see who were still alive. Both the dead and the unconscious were strewn all over the battlefield. Vibhīṣaṇa and Hanumān met each other. Both of them, devotees of Śrī Rāma, grieved to see the fallen princes. At that point, Jāmbavān became conscious. He regained consciousness because of the blessings of his father, Brahmā. Nevertheless, he was finding it difficult to open his eyes. Vibhīṣaṇa went near him and asked, 'Hey noble monkey! Are you alive? Wonderful! Can you recognize me?'

"Jāmbavān replied, 'My eyes are clotted with blood. Hence, I cannot open them. You're Vibhīṣaṇa, aren't you?'

"'Yes, I am.'

"'Is Hanumān alive?'

"Hearing this, Vibhīṣaṇa asked in surprise, 'Why are you inquiring about Hanumān, and not Rāma and Lakṣmaṇa? Do you have such great affection towards him?'

"Jāmbavān said, 'It's not that I'm unconcerned about the princes, but right now, we need Hanumān. The lives of everyone else depend on him.'

"Hearing Jāmbavān's voice, Hanumān rushed happily to him and said, 'Here I am, alive and well!'

"Jāmbavān was overjoyed. He said, 'Hey, Vāyuputra! There is one way to save Rāma, Lakṣmaṇa and all the monkeys lying around unconscious. Only you can do it. Travel to the Himālayas. Near Kailāsa is the Ṛṣabha Mountain. Four divine medicinal herbs, namely *Viśālyakariṇi*, *Sandhānakariṇi*, *Suvarṇakariṇi* and *Mṛtasañjīvani*, grow on top of this mountain. These herbs are imbued with the power and energy of the sun. Go fast, collect these herbs, and bring them back. They have the power to awaken everyone.'

"Hearing this, Hanumān set out at once. Standing on top of the Mahēndra mountains, he roared mightily. The land of Lanka, the rākṣasas, the mountains and even the ocean shuddered at the power of his roar. Then he leapt high towards the north. Within seconds, Hanumān reached the Himālayas, travelled past the ranges, landed in Kailāsa and saw the Ṛṣabha Mountain. Hanumān stood still, astounded by the splendour and majesty of the Kailāsa mountain peak.

"In the meantime, Rāvaṇa, who had secret spies and messengers everywhere, had learnt that Hanumān had gone to procure medicinal herbs. He became fearful. He sat thinking for some time. Finally, he devised a way to stop Hanumān. He had an uncle named Kālanēmi, who was a skilful conjurer. Rāvaṇa went to Kālanēmi and described how the battle had unfolded. 'Rāma, Lakṣmaṇa and the monkey army are lying dead on the battlefield. Indrajit has returned victorious to his palace. If Hanumān brings the medicines back, he will revive them. This must not happen. You must stop Hanumān's return journey.'

"'How can I do that?' asked Kālanēmi.

"Rāvaṇa said, 'There is a way. Assume the guise and manners of a sage and position yourself along his path. As Hanumān has great respect for sages, he will prostrate to you. Talk to him about God and spirituality. He will stay and listen to you. The medicinal herbs become ineffective if there is a delay in administering them.'

"Though Kālanēmi was a rākṣasa, he was knowledgeable about God and matters of the Self. Above all, he desired peace. Although he was very scared of Rāvaṇa, Kālanēmi thought if he counselled Rāvaṇa, hopefully, his nephew would listen to and obey him, his uncle.

Kālanēmi spoke in great length about how transient life on earth was. He then talked about the glory of Rāma's name and of its power to destroy sins from previous lives. All one had to do was to chant the name of Rāma with love and devotion, and one would be purified. He advised Rāvaṇa, 'Abandon your enmity towards Rāma. Pray to him with devotion. Your life will become auspicious.'

"Hearing this, Rāvaṇa became terribly angry. 'I shall first slice you into pieces before doing anything further!' Saying so, he unsheathed his sword.

"Kālanēmi said, 'Don't! I shall do as you say. But this war will definitely destroy you. I shall gain Liberation.'

"Kālanēmi then conjured a hermitage along the route Hanumān was taking to the Ṛṣabha Mountain. He transformed his appearance into that of a sage and conjured up disciples and servants. When Hanumān saw the āśram, he decided he would visit the sage and quench his thirst before travelling on to pick up the divine herbs. The hermitage was beautiful, with many fruit-bearing trees. He saw the sage worshipping Lord Śiva. Hanumān prostrated humbly before the sage and told him that he was a servant of Lord Rāma. He informed the sage that he was on an errand for his Lord. He was thirsty and wanted to know if there was a lake nearby where he could quench his thirst.

"Kālanēmi said, 'With my eyes of knowledge, I can see Rāma, Lakṣmaṇa and the monkeys rising from the battlefield in fine fettle. Drink the water from my *kamaṇḍalu* (water-pot) to quench your thirst.'

"Though Hanumān believed him, he said that the water from the small kamaṇḍalu would not quench his thirst, and wanted to drink from a lake or a river instead. Kālanēmi conjured up a Brāhmin and asked him to lead Hanumān to a water source. He asked Hanumān to return after drinking the water, so that he could give him a mantra that would help him quickly identify the herbs and bring them back. He also asked Hanumān to drink the water with his eyes shut.

"Hanumān entered the deep water source that the Brāhmin showed him, closed his eyes, and started drinking the water. A huge fish came up to gobble him. Actually, Hanumān had opened his eyes a little and seen the fish with its mouth wide open. He grabbed the fish and tore it into two.

"A divine light arose from the fish, which transformed itself into an *apsara* (celestial nymph). The apsara said, "I am an apsara named Dhanyamāli, who became a fish as a result of a curse by a sage. You have released me from the curse. Let me tell you something: it is Kālanēmi who is sitting in the āśram dressed as a sage. His intention is to stop your journey. Go and kill him. Collect the medicinal herbs and return fast. Destroy the entire race of the rākṣasas.'

"Hearing this, Hanumān returned at once to the āśram. Kālanēmi was waiting for him. He said, 'Come, give me the customary *dakṣiṇa* (honorarium) so that I may initiate you into the mantra.'

"Hanumān punched him on his head and killed him. Let us continue the story tomorrow," said Grandma.

Uṇṇi smiled and agreed.

> ***The Lord will help the devotee overcome the obstacles that come his way.***

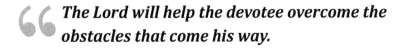

50. Effect of the Elixir, Killing of Indrajit

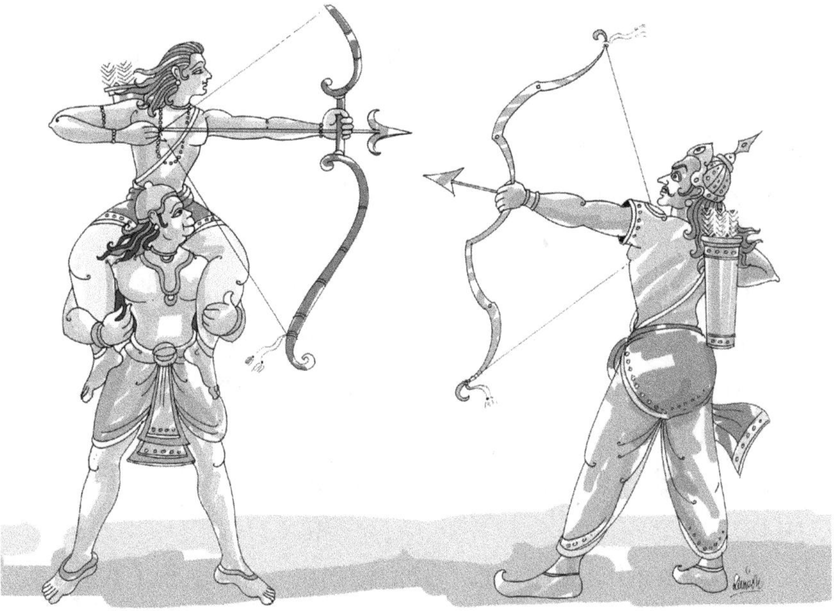

Uṇṇi asked, "Did Hanumān get the divine herbs, Grandma?"

"Of course! There was no way that Hanumān was not going to get the herbs. When he reached Drōṇa Mountain, he bowed down before it. He then sighted the Ṛṣabha Mountain. But how was he going to find the herbs that Jāmbavān specified when the mountain was full of medicinal herbs? He had no time to spare. He uprooted the whole mountain, held it aloft with one hand, and leapt into the air.

"Within minutes, Hanumān landed with the mountain, in front of Śrī Rāma. As the air around the mountain was redolent with the fragrance of medicinal herbs, Rāma, Lakṣmaṇa and the monkeys who had fainted were revived when they breathed in that air.

"But there was a problem: if the mountain remained in the battlefield, it would be impossible to kill the rākṣasas, as they would also come back to life when killed. Therefore, the Lord asked Hanumān to restore the mountain to its original location. Hanumān obeyed the Lord. He placed Ṛṣabha Mountain back where it used to be."

Uṇṇi had a doubt. "Grandma, when Śrī Rāma, Lakṣmaṇa and the monkeys were revived, the fallen rākṣasas must also have come back to life, mustn't they?"

"O Uṇṇi! You're a smart boy! Grandma forgot to mention that Rāvaṇa had ordered the bodies of all the dead rākṣasas to be thrown into the sea. So, there were no dead rākṣasas lying on the battlefield."

Uṇṇi said, "Good!"

Grandma continued, "Sugrīva decreed that no one should stay outside the city of Lanka. 'Most of the rākṣasas have been killed. Destroy the forts and enter the city! Burn the houses and level the wells and moats!'

"The monkeys obeyed his order. They penetrated the forts, burnt the houses, and filled up the deep moats. Once again, Lanka started going up in flames. The city was being reduced to ashes. The rākṣasas and rakṣasīs started howling in terror. There was tumult everywhere. Seeing this, Rāvaṇa became agitated.

"Under the command of Nikumbha, the elite rākṣasas set out to war. The monkeys had been greatly energized by the fragrance of the medicinal herbs. They set upon and massacred the elite forces of the rākṣasa army. Kumbha charged into the battlefield in his chariot, letting fly arrows along the way. Sugrīva picked up the huge rākṣasa and flung him into the sea, but Kumbha swam back, roiling the waters. Sugrīva killed him. Nikumbha then charged into battle but was killed by Hanumān. The remaining rākṣasas fled in terror from the battlefield and informed Rāvaṇa of the death of Kumbha and Nikumbha.

"Rāvaṇa began to feel frightened. He sent Makarākṣasa, a cunning and strong rākṣasa, into the battlefield. Makarākṣasa rained arrows of fire down on the monkeys. Seeing that the monkeys were losing their confidence, Lord Rāma took Makarākṣasa on. The two fought for a long time, a fight between equals, it seemed. Finally, Rāma used the Āgnēyāstra to kill the brute.

"Indrajit had returned to his palace after knocking down Śrī Rāma and the monkey army. When he heard that Rāma and the monkeys had been revived and had killed the most able rākṣasas, he became furious. He attacked all the monkeys who had entered Lanka and threw them out. He consoled his father, 'Be calm. There is no need for worry.' Then he set out again for the battlefield, with a huge army under his command.

"Seeing him advancing, Lakṣmaṇa said, 'Brother, this conjurer will make himself invisible again and rain arrows down on us, and we will fall unconscious yet again. Why don't you release the Brahmāstra and destroy the whole race of the rākṣasas?'

"The Lord said, 'We cannot use the Brahmāstra against those hidden while they are fighting. We should also not use it against those who are not armed. It is against dharma. Nevertheless, we shall defeat Indrajit in battle.'

"Indrajit was looking thoughtful. Suddenly, he returned to Lanka. He conjured up a form of Sītā, seated that form beside him in his chariot, and rode into the battleground. Seeing this, even Hanumān became confused, not knowing what to do. Then, in front of all the monkeys, Indrajit severed Sītā's head, causing blood to spill everywhere.

"Hanumān, convinced that Indrajit had murdered Sītā Dēvī, left the battlefield in despair. He informed Lord Rāma of what had happened. Śrī Rāma fainted. Lakṣmaṇa and Hanumān tried to revive him. Vibhīṣaṇa, who was witnessing all this from afar, came to the Lord, laughing merrily. He said, 'Indrajit conjured up a form of Sītā Dēvī — Māyāsītā. How can anyone destroy Dēvī? Indrajit is trying to buy time so that he can go into Nikumbhila Cave to conduct a fire sacrifice. This was his ruse to buy time."

Uṇṇi asked his grandmother, "What is Nikumbhila?"

"Nikumbhila is a place where sacred fire rituals were carried out. The idol of Bhadrakāḷī in this cave is known as Nikumbhila. Indrajit had to be stopped from performing the powerful yajñas. Otherwise, it would be difficult to defeat him. On Vibhīṣaṇa's advice, Lakṣmaṇa, Angada, Hanumān, Vibhīṣaṇa and others entered the Nikumbhila Cave. It was not easy to enter the cave, which was closely guarded by rākṣasas. The rakṣasas were killed with rocks and trees. Hearing the uproar, Indrajit came out and blocked Hanumān's way. Vibhīṣaṇa said, 'His yajña has been interrupted. Fight him now!'

"Hanumān lifted Lakṣmaṇa onto his shoulders so that he could attack Indrajit. Lakṣmaṇa started releasing arrows. Indrajit retaliated fearlessly. When he saw Vibhīṣaṇa, Indrajit shouted, 'How can you join our enemies and destroy the rākṣasa race?'

"Vibhīṣaṇa answered him calmly, 'I am trying to save our race by serving Śrī Rāma. On the contrary, you are determined to destroy each member of our race.'

"A fierce battle followed. Indrajit's arrows made deep wounds in Lakṣmaṇa's body. Nevertheless, Lakṣmaṇa fought on, destroying Indrajit's chariot and killing his horse. With the aid of powerful magic, Indrajit withdrew and returned in an instant with a new chariot and charioteer. The fierce fight lasted three days. On the third day, Lakṣmaṇa focused his mind on Lord Rāma, let fly the Indrāstra, and severed Indrajit's head. The Indrāstra sped on towards the sea, cleansed itself of the enemy's blood, returned and slipped back into Lakṣmaṇa's quiver.

"The dēvas, sages and apsaras were greatly relieved. Lakṣmaṇa returned with the monkeys and prostrated in front of Śrī Rāma, who embraced his younger brother and praised him. 'You have performed an impossible feat. Now, unable to bear the pain of his son's death, Rāvaṇa himself will come out to fight!'

"They waited for Rāvaṇa's arrival."

Rules governing war must not be violated. Doing so is unrighteous.

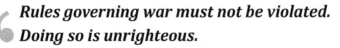

51. Lament of Rāvaṇa, Obstruction to his Hōma

Grandmother continued with the narration of the *Rāmāyaṇa*. "Listen, Uṇṇi. When Rāvaṇa heard that his son had been killed, he fell down in a swoon. When he regained consciousness, he started lamenting. 'My son! How can I bear this sorrow? Why should I go on living? Oh my son!'

"Then he began to roar with anger. Sītā was the sole reason for his misfortunes. Only if he killed her and drank her blood would his anger abate. He ran to the Aśōka Grove where Sītā was sitting. When She saw him coming, red with fury, She began chanting, 'Rāma! Rāma! Rāma! Rāma! Rāma!' Among the rākṣasas guarding Her, there were a few whose hearts were filled with goodness. One was a rākṣasa named Supārśvan, who was also very intelligent. He warned Rāvaṇa, 'O Lord, do not kill a woman now. It will make you infamous and bring terrible misfortune upon you. You have unrivalled skills in warfare and mastery over all fields of knowledge. Go and fight with your enemy. Defeat Him in the battlefield. That should be the next and rightful step. I am with you.'

"Rāvaṇa's anger abated. Accompanied by his rākṣasas, he went to the battlefield. His body became completely wounded by Śrī Rāma's arrows. He retreated to his palace, fearful and despondent, closed the doors and sat down. Then he went to Sage Śukra, the Guru of his clan, and bowed low before him. He said, 'O Master! I am unable to handle the continuous defeats by my enemy anymore. Kumbhakarṇa and Indrajit have been killed. What should I do? Please advise and bless me.' He remained standing humbly before Sage Śukra.

"The sage advised him kindly, "Conduct a *hōma* (religious fire ceremony) at once. Go at once and find a secret place. Conduct a secret yajña therein. I shall tell you the mantra to be chanted as you perform the yajña. From the ritual fire, you will receive divine weapons that will make you invincible.'

"As advised by his Guru, Rāvaṇa found a secret cave, which he entered. As he performed the hōma, he chanted the mantra that his Guru imparted to him. Vibhīṣaṇa, Rāvaṇa's younger brother, knew all the ways of his elder brother. When he saw smoke rising into the skies, he told Rāma, 'O Lord, look up into the skies. Rāvaṇa has started performing a hōma. If he completes it, no one will ever be able to defeat him in war. Therefore, please ask the monkeys to obstruct the hōma at once.'

"Sugrīva ordered the monkeys to hinder the hōma. At once, the monkeys started destroying the surrounding fortifications. They also killed the horses, elephants and guards. But they were unable to find the place where the hōma was being conducted. It was a secret cave, remember?"

"Then how did they discover the cave, Grandma?"

"Vibhīṣaṇa's wife, Saramā, was there. She silently pointed out the exact spot to them. The monkeys saw an opening blocked by a large stone. Angada pulverized the big rock and all the monkeys trooped inside. Uṇṇi, I needn't tell you the damage that a tribe of rampaging monkeys can cause. They killed the servants, poured all the sacred items stored for performing the hōma into the fire, and started hitting, biting and scratching Rāvaṇa. Hanumān snatched the ladle used to pour ghee into the sacrificial fire from Rāvaṇa's hand. Still, Rāvaṇa sat unmoved, deep in meditation, his mind set upon winning the war. When they saw that Rāvaṇa sat unmoved in the midst of all this chaos, the monkeys caught hold of Maṇḍōdarī, Rāvaṇa's wife. They snatched the ornaments from her body and started to rip away her garments. In fear, Maṇḍōdarī shouted to Rāvaṇa, 'O Lord of Lanka, don't you see the monkeys harming me? O fool! You sit unmoved while your enemies harm your own wife. What sin have I committed to be thus insulted? Fool, have you no shame or dignity?'

"Unable to bear the cries of his wife, Rāvaṇa jumped up and rushed towards the monkeys. They released Maṇḍōdarī and ran back to Rāma. They informed Him that they had disturbed Rāvaṇa and stopped the hōma.

"Rāvaṇa told Maṇḍōdarī, 'Consider everything to be God's will. Wipe away the sadness from your heart. I am starting out for war. Either I will kill Rāma, Lakṣmaṇa and the army of monkeys and come back victorious, or Rāma will kill me. If I am defeated and killed, kill Sītā at once. Then jump into the fire, abandon your body, and attain liberation.'

"With great alarm, Maṇḍōdarī said, 'Do not think, even for a moment, that you will win the war. Śrī Rāma is the incarnation of Lord Nārāyaṇa. I understand that He was born to kill you. You caused all our sons to be killed. The reason for all this is your treacherous abduction of Sītā. Therefore, return Sītā to Rāvaṇa. Rāma is infinitely compassionate. He will forgive you for all your sins. Hand the country over to Vibhīṣaṇa. Let us go and live in the forest, meditating in peace for the rest of our lives.'

"But Rāvaṇa would not heed Maṇḍōdarī's wise words. He came up with an explanation for his continuing wickedness. 'It is not right to go and meditate in the forest when all our kin have been killed. Things might not turn out as we plan. Such is the law of nature. I am starting out to war. Know that if Śrī Rāma kills me, I shall reach His abode, Vaikuṇṭha!'

"With great enthusiasm, Rāvaṇa set out to fight."

> ***The strong ego of some people destroys their wisdom and engulfs them in spiritual darkness. Only when they face unfavourable circumstances will they remember God and the laws of nature.***

52. Battle between Rāma and Rāvaṇa

The oil lamp was lit in the pūjā room. Uṇṇi and Māḷu sat facing Grandma. Uṇṇi expectantly said, "Grandma, finally Rāma and Rāvaṇa are going into battle. It will start soon, won't it?"

"Yes, Uṇṇi, the great war was finally going to start. Rāvaṇa reached the battlefield, a huge army marching behind him. You might wonder from where Rāvaṇa procured such a mighty and well-armed military force, as more than two thirds of the rākṣasas in Lanka had already been killed or mortally wounded. You see, Rāvaṇa had kept a strong contingent of cruel rākṣasas, ready and equipped for dangerous emergencies, in *Pātāḷa*, the netherworld. When Rāvaṇa summoned them, they arrived on earth. This heartless contingent advanced like the sea into the battlefield. The monkeys became frightened as wave after wave of the seemingly never-ending ranks of enemy forces marched into the battlefield.

"Śrī Rāma told the monkey army, 'I don't want any one of you to face them. You will be in grave danger. I shall face this army myself.' Śrī Rāma donned His armour and penetrated the ranks of the rākṣasa army.

"Listen, dear Uṇṇi, to the tactics the Lord used to fight. He assumed countless forms so that each rākṣasa faced a Rāma and experienced the Lord fighting with him. How can I adequately describe the great battle? The relentless rain of arrows that rent the air was so dense and powerful that it was difficult to discern whether it was night or day, land or water. The rākṣasas started getting decimated, and headless corpses began to litter the battlefield. Millions and millions of them lay dead on the ground. A river of blood flowed thick and strong. Ghouls came to feast on the blood, and vultures, crows and wolves, to gorge on the carcasses. In a few hours, the Lord massacred all the rākṣasas.

The dēvas, traversing the skies, sang hymns in praise of the Lord. The dense darkness lifted and the air became clear. Śrī Rāma was shining with the brilliance of the sun. Hanumān, Lakṣmaṇa, Sugrīva and Vibhīṣaṇa watched with wonder as the Lord single-handedly annihilated the army of fierce rākṣasas.

Loud wails from the families of the dead demons made Lanka shudder. Their laments were interlaced with imprecations against Śūrpaṇakhā and Rāvaṇa, the sister for instigating the brother to abduct Sītā. They cried in anguish, 'We have to bear the consequences of Rāvaṇa's wicked deeds! Vibhīṣaṇa had warned him, but the despicable tyrant did not heed words of advice!'

"Hearing the laments of his subjects, Rāvaṇa felt sad. He set out for the battleground with Virūpākṣa, Mahōdara and Mahāpārśvan, who were powerful rākṣasas. They saw many bad omens on the way.

"A fierce battle ensued. Sugrīva killed Virūpākṣa and Mahōdara. Angada killed Mahāpārśvan.

"Seeing all his commanders dying on the field, a depressed Rāvaṇa came to the battlefront. A spate of arrows whizzed past him on either side. Rāvaṇa had a vast array of divine weapons with him, including *Tāmasāstra, Asurāstra* and *Mayadatta Māyāstra*, all very powerful and deadly. The Lord had the weapons needed to destroy or neutralize Rāvaṇa's missiles. His divine arsenal included the *Aindrāstra, Āgnēyāstra* and *Gandharvāstra*. As Rāvaṇa's missiles sped towards Rāma, the counter weapons that the Lord wielded would stop and nullify each one of them. Although Rāvaṇa wounded Rāma's body, the injuries the Lord sustained were nothing compared to the wounds Śrī Rāma inflicted on Rāvaṇa. When Vibhīṣaṇa killed Rāvaṇa's horses, Rāvaṇa became furious. He was about to hurl his spear against his brother when he was attacked by a torrent of arrows from Lakṣmaṇa. A wrathful Rāvaṇa hurled the spear against Lakṣmaṇa, who fell unconscious. Śrī Rāma pulled the spear out from his brother's chest, and commanded the monkeys, 'Take care of my brother. I shall return after killing Rāvaṇa. His time is up. Śrī Rāma and Rāvaṇa will not live together in this world.'"

> ***Even incarnations of God will suffer pain when they face and fight against the power of evil.***

53. Arrival of Agastya, Hymn to Āditya

Grandmother continued her narration of the *Rāmāyaṇa*. "Śrī Rāma and Rāvaṇa started bombarding each other with arrows. The air was so thick with the whizzing of arrows that it seemed as if the clouds were raining arrows. The loud twanging of bow strings resounded in the three worlds.

"As Śrī Rāma fought, His mind was anxious and perturbed. Do you know why, Uṇṇi?"

Uṇṇi said, "Because Lakṣmaṇa was lying unconscious in the battlefield, wounded by Rāvaṇa's spear, which had pierced his chest."

Grandmother said, "Yes Uṇṇi, that was indeed the reason. Even though He was God, Rāma had taken on a human body, and was thus susceptible to human emotions such as joy, sorrow and fatigue. Rāma was unable to bear his grief at the thought of Lakṣmaṇa lying unconscious on the battlefield. He asked Sugrīva, 'Is my brother dead? Grief is overpowering me, my body is becoming drained of strength, I feel helpless and unable to fight.'

"Hearing this, the monkey named Suṣēna said, 'Do not fear, my Lord. Your brother is not in any danger. He has fainted, that's all. Like he has done before, Hanumān has gone to fetch the Viśālyakariṇi herb from the Ṛṣabha Mountain.'

"Hanumān returned in a few minutes with herb in his hand. The reviving medicinal fragrance of the herb revived Lakṣmaṇa. He stood up, went up to Rāma, and bowed down before Him. Rāma's grief vanished. Lakṣmaṇa said, 'Do not tarry any longer, elder brother. Kill the monster!'

"The fight between Rāma and Rāvaṇa resumed, a fast and furious battle between two mighty opponents. Rāvaṇa remained seated in his chariot; Rāma fought from the ground. When Sage Nārada realized that Rāma was finding it difficult to defend Himself and advance against His skilled adversary, he informed Indra. Indra asked his charioteer, Mātali, to go down to earth with his chariot and seat the Lord in it. Mātali was also to guide the chariot in the battlefield.

"When the chariot reached the battlefield, Rāma bowed down before Indra's chariot and then stepped inside. A terrible fight began. In the thunderstorm of arrows that fell, Rāvaṇa's arrows severely wounded Mātali, his horses and Lord Rāma. Vibhīṣaṇa became anxious and sad, seeing Rāma bleeding profusely from deep wounds in His arms and legs. He was fast losing strength.

"Seizing this opportunity, Rāvaṇa lunged at the Lord with a spear. Rāma parried the blow with another spear, causing Rāvaṇa's spear to break into two. Seeing this, Rāvaṇa's charioteer drove the rākṣasa away to a safe distance from Rāma. The charioteer's cowardly act infuriated Rāvaṇa. The charioteer explained that he had acted that way because he did not want Rāma's spear to wound his king mortally.

"The battle resumed after an interval. The air grew dark with the thick traffic of streaking arrows. As the battle progressed, Sage Agastya appeared before Śrī Rāma. The Lord prostrated to the venerable sage, who said, 'Rāma, let me initiate You into the *Ādityahṛdaya* mantra, which will enable You to annihilate the enemy and win everlasting honour. If we chant this mantra daily, all our sorrow will vanish. Within Āditya, the Sun God, one can see all the forces of this universe and the dēvas. This divine mantra eliminates disease and sorrow.'

"Having explained the glories of the Sun God, the Sage imparted the *Ādityahṛdaya* mantra to Śrī Rāma. The Lord bowed down before the sage, His mind clear and radiant. 'Chant this mantra and destroy your enemy!' the sage blessed Śrī Rāma as he disappeared from the battlefield."

> ***Forces of nature, imbued with divinity, can conquer evil. Meditate upon such a divine power.***

54. Death of Rāvaṇa, Coronation of Vibhīṣaṇa

Today, Uṇṇi reached the pūjā room before his mother and grandmother. He lit the oil lamp in front of the picture of Lord Rāma. His mind was eager to hear the story of the battle between valorous Rāma and cruel Rāvaṇa. When his grandmother entered the pūjā room, Uṇṇi asked, 'Grandma, will Rāvaṇa be killed today?"

Grandma smiled fondly at her young grandson and said, "Yes, he will. Now hear me out, Uṇṇi.

"Mātali, Indra's charioteer, steered the chariot enthusiastically. Rāvaṇa was not at all anxious or unsettled. He attacked with confidence. Each side began to unleash a barrage of arrows. Rāma broke the mast of Rāvaṇa's chariot. Rāvaṇa wounded Mātali and the horses. The arch rivals employed all the tactics of war, fighting from near and far, as they clashed again and again. It is difficult to describe the clangour and clamour of the war. The celestial beings watched in wonder and amazement as Rāma and Rāvaṇa fought. The wind stopped in its tracks. The sun was eclipsed by the dust rising up from the battleground. The earth quaked. Gigantic ocean waves crashed against the shores. Even the snakes in the netherworld recoiled in fear.

"Lord Rāma lopped off one of Rāvaṇa's heads and hurled it to the ground. Amazingly, Rāvaṇa sprouted another head! Rāma severed Rāvaṇa's heads 101 times, but each time, a new one would appear. Rāvaṇa thus retained all 10 heads. Lord Rāma remarked, 'He has acquired immense strength from his spiritual practices and meditation.'

"They continued fighting, firing arrows at each other. As the days progressed, Rāma noticed that Rāvaṇa's strength was waning. And yet, Rāma was unable to kill Rāvaṇa. The battle lasted for seven days. On the seventh day, Mātali bowed before the Lord and said, 'O Lord! Attack Rāvaṇa with the Brahmāstra that Sage Agastya gifted you long ago. Rāvaṇa will die!'

"Picking up the Brahmāstra, Rāma remarked, 'You have reminded me rightly!' He closed His eyes and meditated upon the Sun, Fire and Wind gods, enshrining those primal forces inside the formidable Brahmāstra. Infusing the strength of mountains into the arrow, Rāma let it fly.

"The Brahmāstra glowed fiercely, illuminating the earth as it sped along. It pierced Rāvaṇa's chest, penetrated the earth, washed itself clean of Rāvaṇa's blood, and flew back into Rāma's quiver. Rāvaṇa fell, like a tall tree crashing to the ground with a thunderous noise."

Uṇṇi exclaimed excitedly, "Oh! Rāvaṇa was killed!"

Grandmother said, "The jubilant dēvas showered flowers on the Lord's head. The sun shone again. Light poured into all the worlds. The breeze started blowing again. The sages started rejoicing and sang hymns glorifying Lord Rāma. The monkeys celebrated.

"But Vibhīṣaṇa was crying uncontrollably, unable to bear the pain of his brother's death. Rāma consoled him, saying that His arrows had washed away all of Rāvaṇa's sins, and that he would attain heaven for the courageous. Śrī Rāma then advised Vibhīṣaṇa to perform the funeral rites without delay. Maṇḍōdarī, Rāvaṇa's wife, fell on his body, lamenting.

"On Lord Rāma's instructions, a pyre was built from sandalwood and other fragrant materials. Rāvaṇa's body was cremated in the presence of sages and Vēdic scholars. Upon Rāma's instructions, Rāvaṇa was cremated with all the rites performed during the cremation of noble Brāhmins. Rāma consoled the grieving rākṣasa women and urged them to return to their homes.

"Rāma then said, 'Lakṣmaṇa, crown Vibhīṣaṇa King of Lanka!'

"The streets of Lanka were gaily decorated. Against the background of musical accompaniment and escorted by sages and the remaining rākṣasas, Vibhīṣaṇa was ceremoniously crowned and proclaimed King and Ruler of Lanka.

"Vibhīṣaṇa presented Śrī Rāma rare and precious gifts from the rākṣasas. The Lord was pleased because He had accomplished His divine mission: killing Rāvaṇa. He embraced Sugrīva and said, 'O Sugrīva, Rāvaṇa could be killed and Vibhīṣaṇa crowned king only because you and the able monkey army under your command helped me in battle. Of this, I have no doubt.'

"Everyone watched with joy as Lord Rāma embraced the monkey king Sugrīva."

> ***The battle between good and evil started from the Trētā Yuga. Good will prevail ultimately because God is Truth and Righteousness. This is the truth.***

55. Accepting Sītā, Dēvēndra's Hymn

Uṇṇi asked anxiously, "Grandma, did Sītā Dēvī know that Rāma had killed Rāvaṇa?"

"Hear me out, Uṇṇi," said Grandma. "As soon as Vibhīṣaṇa was crowned King of Lanka, Rāma told Hanumān, 'With Vibhīṣaṇa's permission, enter the Aśōka Grove and inform Sītā that Rāvaṇa has been killed.'

"After obtaining permission from Vibhīṣaṇa, Hanumān went to the Aśōka Grove. Sītā was sitting there, drooping with sorrow. Hanumān bowed down before Her and said, 'O Mother! The Lord has killed Rāvaṇa! I was sent here to convey the news to you.'

"Sītā's joy knew no bounds. Her face lit up. She said, Her voice breaking with happiness, 'Vāyuputra, I cannot stay away from Him for even one more moment. Go at once and tell Him so.'

"When Hanumān conveyed Sītā's message to Rāma, He told Vibhīṣaṇa, 'Please see to it that Sītā is bathed, dressed in fine clothing, adorned with golden jewellery, and brought here in a carriage immediately.'

"Old rākṣasīs bathed, dressed and adorned Sītā Dēvī and brought Her in front of Śrī Rāma. The monkeys

jostled to get a glimpse Mother Sītā. The palace guards stopped them, but Rāma told Vibhīṣaṇa to let the monkeys enter. He said, 'Let Sītā come and stand near me so that all may see Her.'

"Sītā alighted from the carriage, walked over to and stood beside Her Lord. Rāma's heart was aglow with happiness, but without displaying his joy, He said, 'O Sītā! I have killed Rāvaṇa and rescued You. It was only by the able assistance of Vibhīṣaṇa and the noble monkeys that I was able to accomplish this. I am aware of Your purity and chastity. But You have lived for a year in Rāvaṇa's palace. Can a husband lovingly accept a wife who has lived in the home of another man for a whole year? Your chastity will be doubted by all!'

"Hearing these bitter words, Sītā was overwhelmed by sorrow. Crying bitterly, She said, 'Do You doubt me? Why do You speak in this manner? How can any man other than You have a place in my heart? My heart hurts as if it has been pierced by arrows. Lakṣmaṇa, dearest brother, prepare a pyre for me at once. My name has been tarnished. Even my noble husband doubts me. I have no wish to live any more. Young brother, prepare a pyre for me!'

"Lakṣmaṇa looked at Rāma, who conveyed His consent silently. Lakṣmaṇa built a pyre. Sītā circumambulated Rāma, Her palms joined together prayerfully, lips chanting His name. Sītā Dēvī approached the flaming logs and said, 'O Lord of Fire, if I have remained true to my husband in word, thought and deed, save me. You are witness to everything. If I have even for a single instant held anyone other than my husband in my heart, reveal the truth!'

"Saying so, Sītā Dēvī entered the fire. Seeing this, Indra, Brahmā and other dēvas appeared. As everyone watched, Agni, the God of Fire, appeared with Sītā, who looked radiant. The God of Fire said, 'O Rāma, please take Your chaste and pure wife back. She never forgot You in word thought or deed!'

"Rāma answered, 'O my Sītā, I always knew that You are pure and chaste. But the world does not know it. I allowed You to enter the fire in order to prove Your sanctity to the whole world. I accept You, the purest in all the three worlds!'

"Dēvēndra and the other dēvas, who were watching everything that happened, sang a hymn glorifying Lord Rāma. Indra said, 'Rāmacandra, whatever you desire, I shall fulfil for You! Please command me!'

"Rāma said, 'I desire to see alive all the monkeys who died in the war to kill Rāvaṇa and reclaim my Sītā.'

"Dēvēndra said, O Lord, You have indeed asked for a noble boon. May all the dead monkeys regain life!'

"With these words, all the dead monkeys strewn around the battlefield got up as if from a deep sleep. Śrī Rāma was pleased. The dēvas returned to *dēva-lōka* (abode of the gods) after singing hymns in praise of Rāma."

> ***The king should maintain a pure and high standing in the hearts of his subjects. Only then will the kingdom remain peaceful and prosperous.***

56. Return to Ayōdhyā

Uṇṇi asked, "Grandma, Rāma's 14-year exile had ended, hadn't it?"

"Yes. Rāma told Vibhīṣaṇa, 'I am leaving for Ayōdhyā as fast as I can.'

"Vibhīṣaṇa replied, 'O Lord! You must be weary after the long battle. Please stay here with me in Lanka while You rest and recover.'

"Rāma said, 'Vibhīṣaṇa, please do not compel me to do so. My younger brother has vowed to jump into a burning pyre if I do not return on time. Until I return and meet him, I am not going to bathe, pray or bother about myself in any way. I am also longing to see my mothers, my Gurus and the people of Ayōdhyā.'

"Vibhīṣaṇa insisted once more. 'Please accept my hospitality before You leave.'

"Śrī Rāma said, 'Treat my monkeys well. Make them happy and content. I shall consider the respect you show them as your worship of and love for me.'

"Vibhīṣaṇa arranged a puṣpaka-vimāna for Śrī Rāma, Dēvī Sītā and Lakṣmaṇa to return to Ayōdhyā.

"Rāma said His farewells. 'Vibhīṣaṇa, rule Lanka as a wise and just king. Sugrīva, return to Kiṣkindhā.'

"When they heard this, Vibhīṣaṇa and the monkeys requested Rāma, 'Please take us with you to Ayōdhyā. We long to witness Your coronation as King of Ayōdhyā.'

"Śrī Rāma happily let them climb into the puṣpaka-vimāna with Him.

"As the puṣpaka-vimāna flew through the skies, Rāma looked lovingly at Sītā. He showed Her all the lands He had traversed to reach Lanka. He said, 'Look Sītā, down there is the city of Lanka. Here is the battlefield where Rāvaṇa and Kumbhakarṇa were killed. Over there is the long bridge the monkeys built. Now we are flying over the kingdom of Kiṣkindhā. This is the spot where Vālī was killed.

"Then, addressing Sugrīva, Rāma said, 'Invite all your subjects, male and female, to come along.'

"The monkey women jumped up in joy when they heard that Śrī Rāma had come with Sītā in the puṣpaka-vimāna, and that they were being invited to be guests at His coronation.

"The vimāna rose up again. Śrī Rāma pointed out to Sītā the places he had wandered in search of Her. He said, 'Below is Śabarī's āśram. Over there is Gōdāvarī River, and nearby is Citrakūṭa. Now we can see River Gangā. Nearby is Guha's kingdom of Śṛngavēra.'

"As She gazed upon all the places Rāma pointed out, Sītā smilingly listened. The vimāna landed in Sage Bharadvāja's āśram. They prostrated before the sage, who was a *trikāla-jñānī*, aware of the past, present and future. The sage blessed Rāma, praised the Lord, and sang His glory. The divine trio and their entourage rested in the āśram. Rāma called Hanumān and said, 'Travel at once to Ayōdhyā and inform Bharata of our arrival. Let Guha also know that we are on the way.'

"Hanumān took on a human form and went to Guha first, alerting him of Rāma's arrival. Then he went to meet Bharata in Ayōdhyā. Bharata, sporting matted locks and garments made of tree bark, was living like a sage and worshipping Śrī Rāma's pādukas, which had been placed as a token of His presence on the throne of Ayōdhyā. Hanumān introduced himself, and then recounted to Bharata all that happened — from Rāvaṇa's abduction of Sītā to the killing of Rāvaṇa in battle, and to the Lord's arrival in Sage Bharadvāja's āśram.

"Bharata embraced Hanumān. He informed Śatrughna that their elder brother was arriving. They began preparations to receive Him. Bharata ordered all the roads that Rāma would be travelling along to be cleared and decorative banners to be hung. Bharata waited impatiently for his brother to arrive."

> ***We can remember with a smile the hard times and sorrows we shared in the past.***

57. Rāma-rājya

As soon as they sat down to hear the narration of the *Rāmāyaṇa*, Uṇṇi said, "So, finally, after 14 years, Śrī Rāma, Sītā Dēvī and Lakṣmaṇa are returning to their own kingdom, aren't they, Grandma?"

"Indeed, Uṇṇi! Bharata instructed Śatrughna to do all that was necessary to welcome their elder brother back from His 14-year exile. The people of Ayōdhyā rejoiced at the news. The city became filled up with people eager to see Śrī Rāma. Streets and homes were gaily decorated.

"With Śrī Rāma's pādukas placed devoutly on his head, Bharata set out by road to welcome the Lord. Śatrughna was beside him. As the whole of Ayōdhyā watched expectantly, Hanumān said, 'Look up into the skies! There the puṣpaka-vimāna is, bearing Śrī Rāma, Sītā, Lakṣmaṇa and the others! Feast on the sublime beauty of this sight!'

"All of them stood with heads bowed down and palms joined prayerfully when they saw the Lord in the vimāna. As the vimāna touched down, tears were streaming down Bharata's eyes. He and Śatrughna ran to Rāma. The Lord tightly embraced the two brothers, whom he had not seen for 14 years. They prostrated before the Lord and bowed down with love and reverence in front of Sītā Dēvī. Lakṣmaṇa hugged Bharata and Śatrughna. Bharata hugged Sugrīva again and again, and said, 'You helped my brother win the war against Rāvaṇa and kill him. You are Daśaratha's fifth son!'

"Kausalyā clasped Rāma to her bosom. Lord Rāma and Sītā bowed before the three mothers. Sugrīva and the others also prostrated before them.

"With great devotion, Bharata placed the pādukas before Śrī Rāma's feet and said, 'I have ruled Ayōdhyā with Your grace and blessings for the last 14 years. Today, I am entrusting the kingdom back to You. Protect us, the kingdom and this earth!'

"Bharata's words and actions touched everyone and made them happy. Then everyone got into the vimāna and left for Bharata's hermitage in Nandigrāma. Lord Rāma then ordered the vimāna to return to Vaiśravaṇa, the rightful owner. Rāvaṇa had seized the vimāna from Vaiśravaṇa. Rāma told the vimāna to come when it was wanted.

"Now, Uṇṇi, I am going to tell you about the grand coronation of Lord Rāma.

"Śrī Rāma and Lakṣmaṇa went to Guru Vasiṣṭha and prostrated at his feet. The mothers and relatives of the princes, as well as the chief ministers arrived. All of them, including Kaikēyī, pleaded with Rāma to assume kingship of Ayōdhyā. The Lord agreed to their request.

"Preparations began to be made for the coronation. The Lord discarded the clothes He had worn in the forest, and cut off His matted locks. After bathing, He donned silken robes befitting a ruler. The royal ladies-in-waiting dressed Sītā in silken finery.

"Rāma was as radiant as Lord Viṣṇu as Sītā stood by His side, radiant as Goddess Lakṣmī. Rāma stepped into the chariot steered by Sumantra and travelled to the palace. Lakṣmaṇa and Vibhīṣaṇa fanned the Lord with the turquoise ceremonial fan and the snow-white ceremonial whisk. Śatrughna held the white ceremonial parasol above Lord Rāma. Sugrīva, Hanumān, Vibhīṣaṇa and others accompanied the royal procession on horses and elephants. Sītā and Tārā accompanied them in covered palanquins borne on the shoulders of strong warriors.

"The procession wound its way through the streets of Ayōdhyā. The women stood on terraces to enjoy the sight of the royal parade. Ayōdhyā was riding the crests of pure happiness!

"The chariot stopped in front of Daśaratha's palace. Rāma alighted from the chariot and went inside. He prostrated before his three mothers. Vasiṣṭha escorted Rāma and Sītā to the jewel-encrusted thrones and seated them in royal splendour.

"Sugrīva and the others performed abhiṣēka to the Lord with the waters of many holy rivers. The dēvas presented the Lord with numerous gifts. The *gandharvas* (celestial musicians) sang hymns of praise. The apsaras danced to celestial music. Lord Śiva and Lord Brahmā sang hymns in praise of Śrī Rāma. They congratulated Him for killing Rāvaṇa. A continuous shower of flowers fell from the skies on Lord Rāma and His consort Goddess Sītā.

"After the abhiṣēka, Rāma formally assumed kingship. He then gifted the learned Brāhmins with gold and other precious gems. He gave the monkeys attractive and divine robes. Hanumān was presented with divine gems. Thus Lord Rāma took great pains to ensure the happiness of each and every one present by giving them what their hearts desired.

"He then gently placed around Sītā's comely neck a pearl necklace of exquisite beauty. Sītā took it off and looked at Rāma with a smile on her face. Rāma said, 'Dēvī, You may present it to the one with whom You are most satisfied.'

'With great compassion, Sītā Dēvī presented it to Hanumān, who prostrated before Sītā and wore it at once around his neck.

"Rāma blessed Hanumān, His great devotee: 'May you live on earth for as long as My tale is told!'

"Guha, who had come for Śrī Rāma's coronation, was also given many gifts by the Lord.

"Hanumān then left for the Himālayas to perform spiritual practices. The Lord blessed Sugrīva and Vibhīṣaṇa, and sent them back to Kiṣkindhā and Lanka respectively, to rule over their lands with wisdom.

"While He ruled Ayōdhyā with Sītā Dēvī, Śrī Rāma performed yajñas like the *Aśvamēdha*. Ayōdhyā was peaceful and prosperous under Lord Rāma's rule. There were no enemy attacks, no diseases, no poverty and no infant mortality. Rains fell on time and trees were well protected. The land was filled with plenty. Happiness shone on the faces of all creatures. Such a land, O Uṇṇi, is called *Rāma-rājya*, a utopian realm!"

Grandma placed Uṇṇi on her lap and caressed him. She said, "Grandma has narrated to you the *Rāmāyaṇa* as well as she could. If there have been mistakes, may Lord Rāma forgive me. Uṇṇi, did you understand the story of the brave Rāma? Both of you, Uṇṇi and Māḷu, heard the story patiently, with interest and enthusiasm. Grandma is very pleased. Uṇṇi, when you grow up, you must read the *Rāmāyaṇa* as Vālmīki wrote it. Will you do that?"

"I will, Grandma!" Uṇṇi hugged his grandmother and kissed her fondly. All three of them, Uṇṇi, Māḷu and Grandma, prostrated before the glowing lamp in the pūjā room.

Hearken to what Amma says about Śrī Rāma:

"For an ideal ruler, governance is an austerity; it is worship of the Divine. It is surrendering oneself for the sake of the world. Because King Rāma constantly upheld a ruler's dharma, His subjects were also righteous. Lord Rāma pervades our social life, our arts and the hearts of

devotees. In this day and age, when rulers are given to corruption, unrighteousness and temptations, the self-sacrificing life of Śrī Rāma is a flaming torch dispelling darkness. We ought to read the Rāmāyaṇa so that we can become like Rāma, become Rāma Himself. Children, may you all be able to do so.

Pronunciation Guide

Vowels can be short or long:
a – as ‘u’ in but
ā – as ‘a’ in far
e – as ‘a’ in may
ē – as ‘a’ in name
i – as ‘i’ in pin
ī – as ‘ee’ in meet
o – as in oh
ō – as ‘o’ in mole
u – as ‘u’ in push
ū – as ‘oo’ in hoot
ṛ – as ri in rim
ḥ – pronounce ‘aḥ ’ like ‘aha,’ ‘iḥ’ like ‘ihi,’ and ‘uḥ’ like ‘uhu.’

Some consonants are aspirated (e.g. kh); others are not (e.g. k). The aspiration is part of the consonant. The examples given below are therefore only approximate.
k – as ‘k’ in ‘kite’
kh – as ‘ckh’ in ‘Eckhart’
g – as ‘g’ in ‘give’
gh – as ‘g-h’ in ‘dig-hard’
c – as ‘c’ in ‘cello’
ch – as ‘ch-h’ in ‘staunch-heart’
j – as ‘j’ in ‘joy’
jh – as ‘dgeh’ in ‘hedgehog’
ñ – as ‘ny’ in ‘canyon’

The letters d, t, n with dots under them are pronounced with the tip of the tongue against the roof of the mouth, the others with the tip against the teeth.
ṭ – as 't' in 'tub'
ṭh – as 'th' in 'lighthouse'
ḍ – as 'd' in 'dove'
ḍh – as 'dh' in 'red-hot'
ṇ – as 'n' in 'naught'
p – as 'p' in 'pine'
ph – as 'ph' in 'up-hill'
b – as 'b' in 'bird'
bh – as 'bh' in 'rub-hard'
m – as 'm' in 'mother'
y – as 'y' in 'yes'
r – as 'r' in Italian 'Roma' (rolled)
ḷ – as 'l' in 'like'
v – as w in 'when'
ṣ – as 'sh' in 'shine'
ś – as 's' in German 'sprechen'
s – as 's' in 'sun'
h – as 'h' in 'hot'
With double consonants the initial sound only is pronounced twice:
cc – as 'tc' in 'hot chip'
jj – as 'dj' in 'red jet'

The Rāmāyaṇa in One Verse

ādau rāmatapōvanādigamanam
hatvā mṛgam kāñcanam
vaidēhīharaṇam jaṭāyumaraṇam
sugrīvasambhāṣaṇam
bālīnigrahaṇam samudrataraṇam
lankāpurīdāhanam
paścād rāvaṇakumbhakarṇṇanidhanam
ētaddhirāmāyaṇam

Śrī Rāma went to the woodland in times olden,
and there killed a deer that was golden.
Rāvaṇa seized Sītā and killed Jaṭāyu, the raptor.
Rāma's and Sugrīva's pact dispatched Vālī, his brother.
There is a sea crossing and the razing of Lanka,
where those slayed included Rāvaṇa and
Kumbhakarṇa.
This, in short, is the story of the *Rāmāyaṇa*.

CPSIA information can be obtained
at www.ICGtesting.com
Printed in the USA
LVHW011317290720
661835LV00006B/625

9 781680 377590